DESIGNING
TRAINING

Alison Hardingham

Alison Hardingham read experimental psychology at Oxford University. Her career in education, human factors, and business psychology has brought her into contact with all kinds of teaching and training. She has designed and delivered a huge variety of programmes, from one-to-one tuition with psychotic children to teambuilding with senior managers, and from basic maths with a class of disaffected adolescents to interviewing skills with engineers. She is a director of Interactive Skills Limited, a human resource consultancy which specialises in management development, assessment, and organisation development. She has written many books on psychology, personal effectiveness, and HR issues. Her CIPD-published titles include *Exercises for Team Development* (1999, co-written with Charlotte Ellis); *Psychology for Trainers* (1998); and *Working in Teams* (1998). She lives in Oxfordshire with her son Ian. She believes in experiencing training as well as providing it to others, and has recently taken up scuba diving, and playing the saxophone.

In the TRAINING ESSENTIALS series leading experts focus on the key issues in contemporary training. The books are thoroughly comprehensive, setting out the theoretical background while also providing practical guidance to meet the 'hands-on' needs of training practitioners. They are essential reading for trainers and for students working towards training qualifications – N/SVQs, and Diploma and Certificate courses in Training and Development.

Other titles in the series

Creating a Training and Development Strategy Andrew Mayo

Cultivating Self-Development David Megginson and Vivien Whitaker

Delivering Training Suzy Siddons

Developing Learning Materials Jacqui Gough

Evaluating Training Peter Bramley

Facilitation Skills Frances and Roland Bee

Identifying Training Needs Tom Boydell and Malcolm Leary

Introduction to Training Penny Hackett

The Chartered Institute of Personnel and Development is the leading publisher of books and reports for personnel and training professionals, students, and all those concerned with the effective management and development of people at work. For full details of all our titles, please contact the Publishing Department:
tel. 020-8263 3387
fax 020-8263 3850
e-mail publish@cipd.co.uk
The catalogue of all CIPD titles can be viewed on the CIPD website:
www.cipd.co.uk/publications

TRAINING ESSENTIALS

DESIGNING TRAINING

Alison Hardingham

CHARTERED INSTITUTE OF PERSONNEL AND DEVELOPMENT

First published in 1996
Reprinted 1997, 2000

Design and typesetting by Paperweight
Printed in Great Britain by
The Cromwell Press, Wiltshire

British Library Cataloguing in Publication Data
A catalogue record for this book is available from the
British Library

ISBN
0-85292-644-8

Chartered Institute of Personnel and Development, CIPD House,
Camp Road, London SW19 4UX
Tel.: 020 8971 9000   Fax: 020 8263 3333
E-mail: cipd@cipd.co.uk   Website: www.cipd.co.uk
Incorporated by Royal Charter. Registered charity no. 1079797

Contents

This book is dedicated to the family where I began – to Mum, Dad, and Heather. There is a lot of me in this book, and a lot of me comes from them.

Introduction

I have been designing and delivering training for many years now. It is an activity that always excites my interest and always puts me on my mettle, because training is, more than any other activity, about people, and about the unpredictable, uncontainable, immeasurable, potential of people. I have designed training that has worked like a dream for one group but failed miserably with another. I have seen the same individuals captivated and inspired by one training element, and then (barely hours later) downcast and frustrated by another.

So in this book I have articulated what I have learned from both successes and failures, in the hope that it will help you, and the people for whom you design training, to have more of the former and fewer of the latter. To help you use this book as an accessible reference guide as well as an aid to more leisured reflection, each chapter finishes with a bullet-point summary of its key points for someone embarking on a piece of training design.

For beginners in training design, this book should alert you in advance to all the different paths available to you in providing a training solution to an organisational problem. It will also help you to select the best sequence of paths to follow and to avoid the most common and most serious pitfalls. For experienced designers of training, the book will represent a quick survey of familiar terrain, exposing the reasons behind choices you have been making instinctively for a long time. Hopefully it will also intrigue you with some new avenues of possibility.

1 Understanding Training

Introduction

The deceptively simple word 'training' covers a multitude of diverse experiences. Here is just a brief glimpse of that diversity.

- the cross-section of project managers who have just mastered a new system of project control which is likely to improve significantly budgeting and resource allocation throughout their organisation

- 20 recent graduates from all over Europe meeting for a three-day induction into the company they have just joined; the first night finds them in the bar, drinking as much as they can (for free) and discussing sex, politics, and how to climb the greasy pole

- the senior sales executive hanging on a rope at the top of a 35-metre drop, wondering how on earth he managed to let himself in for this 'Developing Leadership Potential' nightmare

- the female manager in a male-dominated industry who, on a 'Women's Assertiveness at Work' programme, has finally discovered she is not alone in the battles she fights daily to be heard

- the secretary attending a one-day course to familiarise herself with the latest update to her company's word-processing software; by lunch-time she is bored and wishing she was back in the office

- the team of engineers who suddenly understand why their meetings are so painful when they begin to explore their personality profiles together on a teambuilding event
- the shy technician who is finding the role plays and feedback exercises on his 'Basics in Management Skills' course almost too much to bear; he doubts whether he's learning much.

In this diversity lie both the opportunity and the problem in designing training. There are so many possible training approaches to any organisational or individual training need. So there are few needs for which solutions cannot be found, there is little risk of being repetitive or limited in providing training (as long as the designer continues to be imaginative and resourceful) and if a particular solution does not work, it will not be difficult to find an alternative.

But in the face of such diversity, how can training designers begin to make choices? Is there not a risk that they will fall back on old favourites and on the style which comes naturally, simply because they cannot get their minds around the range of options available?

In this first chapter, we take a 'helicopter' view of training: we pull back from it in order to see it more clearly and not be overwhelmed by the diversity of its detail. By doing this, we arrive at a conceptual framework for under-standing training, and also at a systematic way of 'positioning' any particular training requirement so that it becomes easier to make the right choices on how to meet that requirement. We will find that meeting the requirement depends critically on balancing the needs of the organisation and those of the individuals participating in the training.

Doesn't 'training' belong in the circus?

When I began training and designing training some 10

years ago, I was puzzled. I had just acquired a couple of well-meaning but boisterous dogs, and was diligently attending 'dog training classes' with them every week. I wondered why the word 'training' was used both for disciplining so-called dumb animals and for helping intelligent human beings achieve their potential at work. The two activities seemed on the face of it so much further apart than did 'training' from, say, 'education'. I discussed this paradox with a colleague. 'Why do we call it "training", not "education"?' Her immediate response was, 'Because it's about changing behaviour.'

This seems to me now, on more experienced reflection, to contain more than a grain of truth. Usually what organisations and individuals are looking for from training activities is a demonstrable change in behaviour. Examples would be faster typing, active listening to subordinates (whereas before there had been only telling and interrupting), consultation of people who had not been consulted before, and stammer-free delivery in presentations. It is often enough for *education* to 'broaden the mind', to increase knowledge and understanding without any necessary or immediate evidence of behaviour change. *Training* which produced no such evidence would be rapidly discontinued.

So here is the first key point about the nature of training. At its root, it is about changing people's behaviour. And behaviour change is not easily accomplished. So this understanding of training leads us immediately to confront one of its central challenges, a challenge that is addressed throughout the rest of this book.

There are a few other key characteristics of training that we need to recognise at the outset. Again, they can be identified in contrast with general education (Table 1 on page 4).

Table 1

DIFFERENTIATING CHARACTERISTICS OF EDUCATION AND TRAINING

Education	Training
▪ predominantly for children and young people	▪ predominantly for adults
▪ general rather than specific learning objectives, eg to learn French, Geography, Maths	▪ often very tightly focused learning objectives, eg to learn how to conduct an appraisal interview
▪ 'normal', ie often what everyone in a particular age group is doing	▪ 'special', ie time is taken off 'normal' work activities to do it
▪ emphasis is on knowledge transfer	▪ emphasis is on behaviour change

The central challenges of training

The nature of training as described in Table 1 defines its challenges. They are:

▪ to find a way of facilitating change in adults, whose patterns of behaving and ways of viewing the world are established

▪ to motivate learners to learn to someone else's agenda; to encourage experimentation, exploration and development in a learning context that often smacks more of control than of liberation

▪ to demonstrate that the learning is relevant, important, and valuable to individuals who are already skilled and experienced, when some of those individuals feel that they have been forced to take time out from the 'real world' to undergo 'remedial education'

▪ to bring about long-lasting change in behaviour by means of a finite intervention; to ensure that change continues outside the training context.

These challenges are not trivial. So why do organisations and individuals embark on training in the first place?

What's in it for the organisation?

In most organisations, in both the public and private sectors, the training budget is considerable. In fact, training has become such a basic fact of organisational life that the fundamental reasons for investing in it are often no longer made explicit. But to understand the challenges and opportunities of training and to design training in a way that meets the former and exploits the latter, we must be explicit about the pay-offs the organisation is expecting.

The skills pay-off

Organisations invest in training to produce a more skilled workforce. In the vast majority of cases, the organisation specifies quite precisely the skills it needs its people to acquire in order better to meet the requirements of their jobs. Skills training includes IT training for an organisation automating many of its processes, project management training for all those new to a project manager role, sales training, and so on through innumerable examples of specialist, technical and management skills. Such training is typically focused on sub-sets of the workforce who need particular skills.

The culture pay-off

Organisations invest in training to change 'the way things are done around here'. Notable examples would be British Airways' programme for all its staff to bring about greater customer awareness and higher standards of service delivery. So-called 'management skills training' is often less about giving managers new skills and more about encouraging a more supportive, people-friendly, working environment. 'Culture change' programmes attack the same objective directly and explicitly. Such training is typically provided for large numbers of employees, cascading down from the top in many cases.

The morale pay-off

Providing access to high quality training is seen as a mark of a 'good' organisation. It is evidence that it values its people. So organisations sometimes increase training provision for purposes of internal PR, and to 'keep' sections of the workforce who might otherwise leave. The big accountancy firms, for example, have problems keeping their newly qualified staff, in whom they have just invested massively to enable them to pass their accountancy exams. With that part of their workforce, the firm's training focus shifts from the skills pay-off (to produce a new supply of chartered accountants) to the morale pay-off (to keep that new supply happy with the firm).

Of course many training programmes are looking for multiple pay-offs – in skills, culture and morale. A recent teambuilding programme in British Aerospace, for example, was intended to give team members new techniques for group problem-solving (skills), encourage more flexible and co-operative working patterns (culture), and raise energy levels after a round of compulsory redundancies (morale). We shall explore the need to be clear about pay-offs in the chapter on setting objectives for training (Chapter 3). For now, it is enough to appreciate more generally what the benefits of training are for organisations.

What's in it for the participants?

(In this book, I shall use the words 'participants', 'clients' and 'interested parties' to refer to three key groups of stakeholders in training. Participants are the people who actually attend the training course; clients are the people who pay for it; and interested parties are simply that - other people who have an interest in the outcome of the training. They will include participants' colleagues, bosses and subordinates.)

There are some key asymmetries in what the organisation is looking for from training, and what the participants are looking for. Balancing their frequently conflicting interests is one of the essential challenges of good training design.

Participants are also interested in skills, culture and morale pay-offs from training. But their emphasis in each case is likely to be subtly different. In terms of skills, participants ultimately want to increase their marketability, inside and outside the company. Also, they want to learn skills that they judge interesting and worthwhile. These may or may not coincide with the organisation's priorities.

In terms of culture, participants will also often be looking for things to change. But all participants will have their own idea of how they should change, and will – at least initially – hope the training convinces others of their views. Few of us attend training programmes hoping to be proved wrong.

In terms of morale, participants do want to leave training programmes feeling that the organisation has made a significant and worthwhile investment in them. But they will often see a training programme as an opportunity to step back from their day to day concerns and make a judgement on how much the organisation deserves their loyalty. So they won't, often, attend with the intention of increasing their own commitment to the organisation. They will attend to find out if they should.

> Pause for a few moments and reflect on training courses you have been on. Which, if any, worked for you? Can you identify long-term benefits from any of them, for you personally? When the training didn't work, why was it? (You will find you are your own best resource in designing training. Think to yourself, as you design, 'How would I feel if I were participating in this?')

The training designer's balancing act

So there you have it. You are designing a training

intervention for an organisation which wants it, crudely put, to make their people do their jobs better. And many of the ultimate recipients of that intervention will have something quite different on their minds when they walk through the door to the training suite. What is more, the people paying your bill are not the people receiving your product. And finally, just in case this isn't challenging enough, the people receiving your product will change the nature of your product and so determine its success or failure by their reaction to and with it.

This is the essence of the training designer's balancing act. You walk the tightrope between your paymaster and your customers. This is what makes training design difficult, and, ultimately, what makes it fun.

What make it possible are the many motivations, wishes, and needs on the participant's part which can operate in your favour. Here are a few of the most important.

- ▌ People like to become more competent. Where behaviour change can be clearly identified as an increase in competence, as defined by the participant, he or she will want to make the training work.

- ▌ People want to have enjoyable sociable experiences. Training is usually conducted in groups. There is a natural potential for enjoying meeting others, networking, catching up with old colleagues, working together in a different and usually more relaxed setting. This potential provides energy to the training process, if you harness it.

- ▌ People enjoy a change, a break from the daily routine. There is often anticipation and interest in a training room, or just beneath the surface, waiting to be tapped.

- ▌ People like to compete. On a training programme, this natural competitiveness can be used as another source of positive energy.

- ▌ People need feedback, and get too little during the normal working day. Training involves lots of feedback, and will often engage the participant for this reason alone.

▌ People are basically curious, even when this natural curiosity has been temporarily submerged beneath pressure and the daily grind. On a training programme, there is potentially a lot to be curious about: the training, the other people on the course, the content, the methods, our own reactions. Here is yet another source of positive energy.

Weighing up the training challenge: the 'training frame'

The size of the challenge in any particular piece of training design will depend on the balance of forces working for you and forces working against you. We have just discussed in general terms the most important positive and negative forces. Now we shall look at a way of positioning a training intervention which will alert you to the forces operating for and against that specific intervention. I call it 'the training frame' (Figure 1).

Figure 1

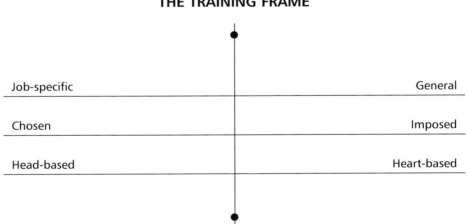

THE TRAINING FRAME

Job-specific	General
Chosen	Imposed
Head-based	Heart-based

The frame comprises three dimensions:

■ *'Job specific' v 'General'*
This dimension is about the nature of the behaviour change the training is required to deliver. At one end of the spectrum is behaviour change highly specific to the participant's job. An example would be training for recruiting managers in the use of a personality questionnaire. They are not required to use the knowledge and skills acquired for anything other than their job. At the other end of the spectrum is behaviour change affecting the whole of the participant's life. An example would be training in understanding and responding to your impact on others. Many 'interpersonal skills' and 'assertiveness' courses are essentially about this.

■ *'Chosen change' v 'Imposed change'*
This dimension is pretty self-explanatory. An example of chosen change would be when individuals decide they want to improve their competence in budgeting and apply to go on a financial management course. An example of imposed change would be if managers sent them.

■ *'Head-based' v 'Heart-based'*
You may be familiar with the well-established 'knowledge, skills, attitudes' categorisation often applied to training content and objectives. When a training intervention is only about imparting knowledge, it is totally 'head-based'. Very few are. An example would be a module in an induction programme on organisational structure, or language skills training (the word 'skills' is deceptive here – it is still essentially about knowledge). When a training intervention is only about changing attitudes, it is totally 'heart-based'. Again, very few are, but examples would be a training programme to sell a new set of 'values' to employees, or a motivational rally by a famous speaker. 'Skills programmes', which constitute the vast majority of training interventions, are usually

a mix of head and heart – head to impart specific techniques and approaches, heart to encourage a willingness to use them. Management skills programmes certainly fall into this category.

How to use the training frame

Imagine you have been asked to design a training course in 'negotiation skills'. Before you begin, you want to know the nature of the training challenge so that you can adapt your design to meet it.

So you ask some questions, and discover the 20 people who are due to attend have just taken on new responsibilities in contract negotiation. They have asked for a basic negotiation skills course before they go on the advanced contract negotiation course the following month, and they are hoping the course will make them familiar with the language, concepts and approaches of negotiation before their true skills development programme on the contract negotiation course. It should also build their commitment to developing good skills themselves. Basically, you are facing a fundamentally job-specific, chosen, head-based challenge (see Figure 2).

Figure 2

THE FIRST NEGOTIATION SKILLS TRAINING EXAMPLE

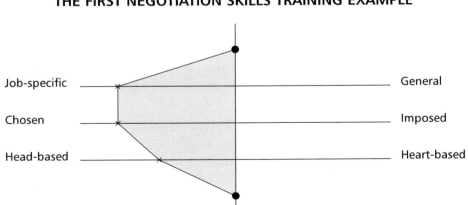

The first thing to say about this challenge is that it is not too great. The shaded area in Figure 2 is mostly to the left of the frame, which means that many positive forces are already working and few negative ones. The job-specific nature of the change taps into the participants' desire to become more competent; the fact they have chosen it reduces the potential conflict between what the organisation wants and what they want; the fact that it's more about knowledge than about attitude (head versus heart) means the forces of habit, custom, and deep-seated preferences are not stacked against you.

In fact, conceptualising the training intervention in this way will lead the training designer to the view that the challenge will lie mainly in the structuring of the content to be clear, comprehensive and interesting, rather than in finding ways to overcome learning barriers in the participants.

Imagine a very different background scenario for the design of a negotiation skills course. The organisation has asked for it because its managers have erected walls between departments, they stonewall colleagues' requests for information, they fail to agree standards and timings for one department's services to another, and their exchanges are characterised by conflict and communication breakdown. The organisation wants this to change. It is sending all managers on the negotiation skills course, in groups of twelve. The managers see no need for the course, they do not see themselves as having responsibilities in negotiation, and so far as they are concerned, structural problems are responsible for the atmosphere of conflict and poor communication. Figure 3 illustrates the training challenge.

Immediately the training designer's challenge is looking more substantial. The shaded area is to the right of the frame. The training intervention is about a general change in management behaviour, it is being imposed and on balance it is more about attitude change than knowledge

Figure 3

THE SECOND NEGOTIATION SKILLS TRAINING EXAMPLE

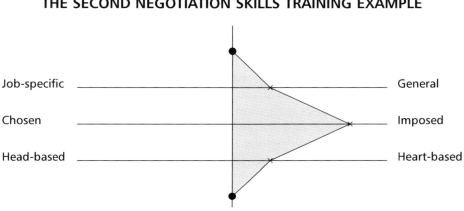

Job-specific	General
Chosen	Imposed
Head-based	Heart-based

transfer. The training designer knows from this analysis that the success of this piece of training will stand or fall by whether the design has allowed for overcoming of objections, and achieving buy-in by the participants. The material on negotiation skills will be less important than the process of discussion and debate about their relevance.

First things first

Because training is primarily about behaviour change and not knowledge transfer, the training designer needs to be most concerned with the learners and much less concerned with what is to be learned. People often go into education out of an enthusiasm for their subject; trainers and training designers are much more likely to be motivated by enthusiasm for people.

The classic mistake in training design is to be seduced by the logic and beauty of the training content, forgetting until later the participants who will receive the training. The training frame we have introduced is one way of ensuring that in our approach to training design we put people first.

The training frame is, if you like, the *science* of putting first things first. There is a second and equally important approach to understanding the nature of the training challenge before you start the training design. I would call it the *art* of putting first things first.

The greatest resource in any training intervention is the group. If you can tap into that resource as a training designer the group will do half your work for you before they even enter the training room. I am not talking here about the process of analysing the precise nature of their training needs. That is of course important, but it is covered in another book in this series (*Identifying Training Needs* by Tom Boydell and Malcolm Leary). I am talking about the process of imagining that group as they approach the training and of tapping into their feelings, values and concerns. Here is how to do it.

Investigating the participants

Often you can find out some useful facts about the people for whom you are designing training – the ultimate participants on your programme. Table 2 details some of the most commonly and generally available facts.

One way of finding out even more facts is to send, or ask the HR department to send, short questionnaires to all future participants before the course is designed. Typical facts such questionnaires ask for are:

- specific individual training needs which the programme could address
- previous ways in which the individual has addressed those needs
- general training history
- career history
- comments on the training they are going to attend.

Use such questionnaires with care. They can infuriate participants – no one much likes completing questionnaires

Table 2

SOME OF THE MOST COMMONLY AVAILABLE FACTS ABOUT PARTICIPANTS

The training they are attending. This is one piece of information you have about everyone. And it is significant. People attending a course on conducting redundancy interviews will have very different sets of concerns, hopes and fears from people attending a course on Microsoft Word.

The extent to which they know others on the course. So are they thinking about people they like and dislike? Will there be networks and allegiances? Or will there by shyness and reserve?

Organisational relationships between people on the course. Will there be power struggles? Worries about being too open, or too critical? Will people be trying to make a good impression? Or score points?

Age. Imagine a group of twenty year olds. Now imagine a group of fifty year olds. And now imagine designing a training course in personal presentation for each group. The courses would be as different as the groups.

Education. Be careful not to take certain educational experiences for granted in your design. Some people, for example, assimilate written information quickly and easily. For others, too much written information is a barrier.

– and so increase the size of the training challenge before you start. Also, I would say, one interview with a single participant, lunch with a group of them, or a visit to their department are all infinitely better ways of understanding them than a stack of questionnaires. Especially when that interview, lunch, or visit is combined with an active and disciplined imagination.

Imagining the participants

■ Find a quiet place, where you can sit comfortably and uninterrupted.

■ Close your eyes.

■ Imagine you are standing at the front of an empty training room. Imagine the emptiness, the peace, the space. Keep imagining this until you feel relaxed and unperturbed.

- Now imagine the door opens and one of the intended participants comes in, expecting the training you are about to design.

- How is he walking? What expression does he have on his face? Where does he look? How is he dressed? Imagine it all, in your mind's eye.

- Is he saying anything? To whom? And what about? Is his voice loud or soft? Imagine the expression, the pitch and volume of his voice.

- How is he feeling? What's on his mind? What successes has he experienced recently? What failures? What uncertainties is he wrestling with? How has he been getting on with his colleagues? With his boss? With the people he manages? What are his priorities? Who's making demands on him? What's he hoping for?

- If you are lucky enough to know actual named individuals who will be attending this training, imagine them coming through that door in turn, and apply the imaginative thinking process to each one. Then reflect on the others, whose names and identities you do not know. Again, using your imagination, see if any additional insights emerge.

- You may know little about the individuals you are designing training for. The more you know, the better equipped you will be to design a good piece of training. But even if you don't know much, the imagining process will help you make the most of what you do know.

But anything you know about the people you are designing training for is gold-dust. Dredge it up and let it feed your imagination.

The relationships between organisation and participants

There is a final factor any training designer must pay attention to in sizing up the training challenge. It is in many ways the single most important influence on that challenge. It is the relationship between the organisation and the participants at the time the participants will walk through the door of the training suite. The worse the relationship, the more difficult it will be for the training to be effective, and the more problems the training designer will have in the balancing act between demands of the paymaster and needs of the participant.

Here are examples of questions to ask when you are imagining (or investigating) the state of that relationship.

- How is the organisation doing, generally? Well, or badly? Are participants likely to be feeling proud of its success or annoyed that their contributions to that success aren't being recognised? Are they likely to be feeling united against the challenges the organisation faces or despondent and disappointed about its failures?

- How is top management viewed? With respect and trust? With realistic consideration? With resentment and mistrust?

- Have there been redundancies recently? Will the participants be feeling under threat? How well have the redundancies been handled?

- Is the organisation united, or are there significant splits or factions? (When there have been mergers or take-overs, there are possibilities of long-lived divisions which run deep.)

- Are the participants satisfied or not with the basic 'hygiene' factors in their working environment (pay, accommodation, resources)?

> What kind of relationship do you have with your own organisation at this point in time? Imagine you are being sent on a training course next week, on, for example, customer care. How would you be feeling about it? Why would you be feeling that way?

In brief

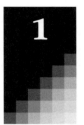

- Training is different from education, and presents different challenges.
- Its key characteristics are that it is intended to produce specific behaviour change, usually in adults.
- The degree and nature of the challenge that a specific piece of training design will present depend on:
  - how different the organisation's and the participants' objectives for the training are (good clues to the size of this difference lie in how specific the training is, how voluntary it is, and whether its focus is on acquiring knowledge or changing attitude)
  - the state of mind and heart the participants will be in when they attend the training
  - the state of the relationship between the organisation and the participants at that time.
- Understanding these key influences before embarking on a piece of training design is the foundation for success. They are best understood by a judicious mix of analysis and imagination.

2 Training Choices

Introduction

In this chapter are pointers to guide the training designer in what I would call 'background choices'. These are choices about:

- programme structure
- venue
- training deliverer(s)
- 'interactive' versus 'distance' learning
- use of IT
- cost.

Whilst these choices are not concerned with the detail of training design, or with the actual content of a training intervention, they can have as much influence on its success as does the detail. Examples of this influence, for good and bad, will be found in the chapter.

In my experience, people who are learning how to design training often neglect these background choices. And when participants are asked to fill in course evaluation questionnaires at the end of a piece of training, the assumption is often made that they can and will judge the training content separately from the venue, the deliverers, and so on. But in fact the participant's experience of a training event is an integrated one. Cramped conditions, poor food, and uncomfortable rooms will influence reaction to the training, interaction with it, and hence the training's effectiveness, in ways too subtle to be avoided, too insidious to be reasoned away. And on the positive side, the training designer often underestimates the size of the helping hand which a good structure, appropriate venue, and intelligently chosen deliverer can give the programme.

In making background choices, the training designer needs to consider the degree and nature of the training challenge (see previous chapter) and the potential of different choices to meet that challenge. We make some of these considerations explicit for the key training choices below.

Programme structure

The fundamental choice in relation to programme structure is whether the training should be modular or not. Contrast, for example, a continuous residential programme of four weeks in length in strategic management, with a modular programme with the same title comprising 10 two-day courses in a year. Both approaches to this particular subject exist, and they both cover similar topics – examples would be elements on leadership, on finance for senior managers, on marketing, on organisational development, and so on.

Modular programmes may also involve project work, which is initiated and reviewed in classroom sessions but which is carried out between sessions, usually in the normal working environment.

A good choice

A large government organisation was undergoing profound change, in order to meet new requirements, standards and regulations imposed on it. Its most senior managers were on the whole long-standing employees, whose skills and attitudes had evolved for an environment very different from that intended for the future. Training in skill areas such as budgeting, business planning, and team management was needed, as was a change of attitude from resentment of change to opportunistic capitalising on change.

This organisation designed a modular training intervention for its top managers. A launch workshop enabled them to profile their strengths and development needs against the requirements of the evolving jobs. They were then able to select from a menu of skills modules to address their development needs. Every two months, a review workshop was held where the managers exchanged news and views on how their development was progressing. They also took the opportunity to discuss issues of broad relevance related to the organisational change which was going on. The workshops proved a forum where they could gain confidence that they were up to the challenge, and come to terms with the changes and their implications.

The modular nature of this training intervention allowed people time to develop, at differing speeds, in some quite fundamental ways. It respected their individuality at a time when they were concerned about being forced into the 'corporate mould'. It was effective.

A bad choice

In another large government organisation, the training requirement was similar. But it was met with a single fortnight-long residential programme for every senior manager, entitled 'Managing Change and Managing Success'. Those who were already committed to the changes enjoyed the programme and gave it high ratings. The 'sceptics' were further alienated by it, and felt trapped by its intensity.

Good and bad choices can be the other way round to these two examples too. I know of an organisation which used the modular approach for senior management skills, but failed because the managers were too busy to keep up the momentum of learning between review workshops. I also know of an organisation which used the 'single hit' approach and made it work extremely well: by making sure that every manager went on the programme in a space of three months, and that every programme ended with commitment to specific actions which were followed up.

How to choose

In considering 'single hit' versus 'modular', you will find the pointers in Table 3 alert you to the key issues.

Table 3

KEY POTENTIAL BENEFITS OF 'SINGLE HIT' AND MODULAR TRAINING

'Single hit'	Modular
∎ simpler to organise, for training providers and participants	∎ scope for many more links between training and work
∎ high intense impact	∎ sustained impact
∎ strong bonding between participants; everyone attends all of it together	∎ people given time to work through a range of reactions and feelings
	∎ people less likely to be required to sit through sessions irrelevant to them personally
∎ may be all that's required, particularly for 'low challenge' training (see Chapter 1)	∎ often the best choice for 'high challenge' training

Venue

Key choices in relation to venue are whether to run training in the workplace or away from it, whether the training should be residential or not, and whether to choose a hotel or a training centre.

> What venues does your organisation typically use for its training? Recall the last course you went on. Did the venue enhance your learning, get in the way of it, or simply fade into the background? Have you ever been to a truly 'awful' training venue? What made it so awful?

Just to underline that there is more to making these choices than the issue of cost, here are a few examples where choice of venue was critical to the success (or failure!) of the training.

Some good choices

- An adequate but spartan local training centre for a population of engineers whose organisation was in financial trouble and had had to make some of the engineers redundant.
- A plush hotel with extensive leisure facilities and gym for a high profile international training event, where networking between participants was as important as any of the other training objectives.
- Training at work for traders in a merchant bank who had to be able to respond immediately to crises in the financial markets.
- Hostel-type accommodation for graduate recruits on an outward bound course.

Some bad choices

- A residential programme for an organisation where equal opportunities was a hot topic. Women with children were too angry to concentrate on the programme initially; one mother insisted on bringing a highly disruptive two-year-old to dinner.
- A hotel mid-way between London and Manchester for an organisation with bases in both cities, and a high degree of touchiness about which base was more

important. Unfortunately the hotel was much more difficult for everyone to get to than a hotel either in London or Manchester!

■ A luxury hotel where lunch was served and took two hours, and dinner took three hours, for a residential programme intended to energise middle managers into becoming 'agents of change' with an intensive series of action-packed tasks!

How to choose

Table 4 lists factors you need to take into consideration in choosing venue.

Table 4

KEY FACTORS RELATING TO CHOICE OF VENUE

■ cost, and perception of cost

■ need to be accessible to colleagues and clients versus need to be uninterrupted

■ need for evening or early morning work, or both

■ extent to which a high degree of bonding between participants is required for the training to be effective

■ relative importance of social time and course time

■ culture and history of the organisation in relation to training venues

■ need for high quality training resources, for example video equipment, one-way mirrors, fully equipped syndicate rooms

■ training 'culture' most appropriate to the course, for example 'business-like', 'celebratory', 'fun', 'tough', unusual and experimental

■ distance participants are prepared to travel

Another way you think about training venue is to consider its potential as an indicator of the values implicit in the training itself. You can either ignore this potential, in which case you run the risk of the venue being at odds with the training in terms of the expectations and atmosphere it sets up; or you can exploit it and use it as a contributor to the training's success. Table 5 gives some examples where training designers have exploited venue to communicate values, to good effect.

Table 5

EXPLOITING THE VALUES IN VENUES

Type of company	Type of training	Values to be communicated	Venue chosen
PR agency	induction	'work hard, play hard'	small luxurious country hotel; very well-stocked bar open till all hours
'big six' accountancy firm	all management skills training	'up to date, business-like, well-resourced'	purpose-built training centre on a university campus
charitable trust	values workshop	'caring for others, responsible stewardship'	local community centre; no bar
merchant bank	teambuilding	'success, achievement, prestige, internationalism'	5 star hotel in Geneva

Training deliverer

The choice of training deliverer needs to be very much part of the process of designing training. In many cases, the designer will be delivering all or part of the training; and I would go so far as to say that most training is best delivered all or part by the designer. That is because no matter how good the briefing, how extensive the tutor notes, the designer will have all sorts of interesting and detailed reasons for constructing the training in the way she has which are inside her head only and not available to others. Also, a key part of delivering training is adapting it to each group as the course evolves (see section on 'Manoeuvrability' in Chapter 5 – pages 64–66). Who is better placed to adapt a programme than the person who designed it in the first place?

There are, however, many interesting options to enhance training delivery. In this section we look at these choices:

▌ one deliverer, or a team
▌ internal deliverers, external, or a mix
▌ specialists, experts and 'gurus'.

One deliverer, or a team

The most important thing to grasp in making this choice is that, if you have two or more deliverers working simultaneously with the group, they are a team. The delivery will have a very different quality from delivery by a single trainer, or by a series of individuals. Table 6 details the key points in that difference.

Table 6

KEY POTENTIAL BENEFITS OF 'LONE DELIVERER' AND 'TWO PLUS'

Lone deliverer	Two plus
▌ participants feel he or she is 'theirs', they confide in and relate to him or her readily	▌ deliverers can work together to win over difficult groups; they are more resilient
▌ consistency of delivery	▌ variety of delivery
▌ deliverer can become 'wallpaper' rapidly, throwing focus onto content	▌ possibility of humour and interest in 'double act'

Internal, external, or a mix

I have heard the view expressed that you use internal trainers when you can't afford external ones. This is far too simplistic, and ignores the particular advantages of internal deliverers. See Table 7.

Table 7

KEY POTENTIAL BENEFITS OF INTERNAL AND EXTERNAL DELIVERERS

Internal deliverers	External deliverers
▌ understand the organisation	▌ bring knowledge of other organisations
▌ are seen as colleagues, 'in it', with the participants	▌ are seen as outsiders, with no axe to grind
▌ are perceived as 'cheap' (hence appreciated and not resented)	▌ are perceived as 'expensive' (hence listened to)
▌ are seen as having channels of communication and influence with management	▌ are seen as neutral

For training which poses a high level of challenge, a mix of internal and external deliverers, judiciously used, gives you the best of both worlds. The combination of internal clout and external credibility can be a winning card, worth more by far than any amount of brilliant presentation of content.

Specialists, experts and gurus

This choice takes things one step beyond the internal versus external debate. Put most straightforwardly, it is about whether you pay more for outstanding delivery skill and exceptional knowledge (or both) and relevant experience.

I have delivered a substantial amount of training for a government organisation which uses a whole range of training deliverers, from 'free' internal trainers, through 'independents' at about £300 per training day, to 'experts' at over £1,000 per training day. I once asked the training manager what decided his choice for any particular intervention. The reply that he gave was stunning in its stark simplicity: 'The greater the training challenge, the more I'll pay.'

Of course the picture is slightly complicated by the fact that some training may not be particularly challenging in the terms that I have already described in Chapter 1, but may only be deliverable by an expensive expert in an abstruse field.

One final point is worth making here. In very challenging training, don't neglect the potential effectiveness of the 'Professor Branestawm' factor – that is, of an obviously very bright and expert individual who makes no concessions whatsoever to the organisational constraints but trains entirely from his knowledge base. Participants can find such individuals captivating and inspirational in their ability quite simply to take them out of themselves and their own organisational mire. I know a specialist in the physiological basis of stress who is used on stress management workshops for that reason. Participants call her 'Doctor Stephanie' and she blinds them with the science of stress. Her unusual and appealing approach gets them over their resentment at being sent on a stress management workshop when they believe what the organisation should really be doing is making their working day less stressful.

'Interactive' versus 'distance' learning

Interactive learning implies people learning together. Distance learning implies people learning on their own, using workbooks, videos, correspondence with tutors, and IT. Distance learning has been steadily increasing in popularity.

There is one key question here: how necessary is interaction with others to achievement of one or more of the training objectives? If it isn't necessary at all, distance learning has several advantages: participants can do it at their own pace, they can fit it into their own schedules, they are likely to take a high degree of personal responsibility for their own learning, and, of course, it is relatively cheap.

Because training is, however, mostly about behaviour change not knowledge acquisition, it is rare that no interaction is required. Behaviour change depends on feedback and coaching. You certainly don't get enough feedback from a book for the more challenging types of behaviour change; nor do you get the emotional support of a good coach. What is often worth considering is a basically interactive programme with some distance learning elements – for preparation and/or follow-up work.

Use of IT

Table 8 summarises the considerable benefits IT can bring to a training programme.

Table 8

KEY POTENTIAL BENEFITS OF USING IT IN TRAINING

- a strong implicit message about the state-of-the-art, well-resourced nature of the training provision

- support for/consistency with an organisational focus on using IT more effectively

- IT skills improved as a by-product of the training

- greater flexibility of presentation of content (for example, complex spreadsheets can be manipulated in business case studies, personality questionnaires can be scored and profiled automatically)

- removal of the barrier to learning which, for some people, occurs whenever they are confronted by a 'human teacher'; machines can take the personal element out of success and failure

There are three significant problems with using IT:

▮ logistics and expense (and the risk of people being preoccupied with a 'bug in the system' rather than with the training content!)

▮ many people's fear of, or incompetence with, IT which will get in the way of their learning

▮ the risk that even though they are learning in a group, participants will become individualistically focused on their own PC, the group dynamic will be reduced or lost, and they might as well be doing distance learning.

For any training intervention, the training designer needs to weigh up these pros and cons for the specific participants and the specific training objectives. At the moment, the cons tend to outweigh the pros for all but the most technologically motivated organisations or the most IT-related training objectives. My guess is, however, that the first two problems listed above will become less and less significant over the next few years, and the balance will tip the other way. IT will become an increasingly normal resource in training programmes.

> Whether you design IT into your training or not will probably have as much to do with how comfortable you feel about it as with the arguments in this section. So stop to consider your own attitude to IT. Will your feelings be a barrier to using IT effectively? If so, how could you change them? Or who could help you in designing training which needs an IT component?

Cost

When do you deviate from the simple maxim 'do it as cheaply as you can'? If you have thoroughly explored all the options and all their pros and cons, understood the training objectives, and are confident that these can be met whichever of the possible design solutions you go for, then the answer is 'hardly ever'.

But this is a big 'if'. A training intervention is never perfect, and it is hard to decide what constitutes 'good enough'. So my advice on cost would be: decide on a budget which corresponds to the value of the training to the organisation if it succeeds. (In other words, is this a 'nice to have' or a 'need to have', from the organisation's point of view? Will it guarantee the organisation's survival, or just mean one or two people who might have left will stay? Use your best judgement to make an approximate estimate of value.)

Then, once you have allocated most to the most important interventions and least to the least important, and stayed within overall budgetary constraints, you design the best you can for that budget. Otherwise you will always end up spending more than you can really afford, because you are seduced by all the training goodies in the sweet shop. Or, just as unfortunately, you will always buy cheap and never find out how much the more 'expensive' training interventions can do for you.

One last word on cost: sometimes you should make the training solution very expensive just to get people's attention. I know of teambuilding sessions with boards and senior management teams that cost a lot not just because they are highly challenging, but also because cost is one way to get them taken seriously.

In brief

- Before design proper is even begun, background choices need to be made which will have a big impact on the effectiveness of the training.
- The most important of these choices are concerned with programme structure, venue, training deliverer(s), 'interactive' versus 'distance' learning, use of IT and cost.
- These choices all bring different potential benefits (and costs). They have to be made in the light of the

particular participants who will be attending and the specific training objectives which have been set.

■ The degree of challenge a particular training intervention poses is also fundamental to many of these choices. Crudely put, more challenging training will often demand more complex programme structures, a venue consistent with the values the training implies, a team of training deliverers rather than one on his or her own, and a highly interactive environment.

3

What Difference Does it Make?

Introduction

Training objectives are succinct statements of what a piece of training is intended to achieve. Table 9 gives some illustrative examples. (I am not making any comment here on how 'well formed' these examples are. That is for later in this chapter.)

Table 9

EXAMPLES OF TRAINING OBJECTIVES

The purpose of this programme is:

▌ to enable participants to conduct effective appraisals

▌ to introduce the new report-writing standards

▌ to identify participants' strengths and development needs in the project manager role

▌ to increase participants' effectiveness and confidence as team leaders

▌ to improve levels of customer service

▌ to train participants in the use of an analytical troubleshooting methodology

Most training interventions have more than one objective. They usually have a set of linked objectives, such as to:

▌ identify ways in which the team is working effectively together

■ identify how the team needs to work differently to be more effective

■ plan how to achieve the necessary changes

■ increase each team member's awareness of their impact on others in the team.

The above are a set of linked objectives which would be typical of a teambuilding programme.

Setting objectives is generally considered the single most important step in designing training. I would certainly consider it such. Not only is it fundamental in focusing the training designer's mind and achieving an unambiguous contract between training designer and customer. It is also the key to winning the participants' commitment.

Because training is outside 'normal' working activity for most participants (see Chapter 1, Table 1), they will typically approach training at least a little confused, apprehensive and annoyed. Their confusion stems from not knowing what to expect from the training. This is in stark contrast to their ordinary working experience, where they do know what to expect. Training objectives, intelligently researched, carefully worded, effectively used, will reduce confusion by giving the participants clear expectations.

The participants' apprehension stems from a feeling that they may be exposed in training, that what they do not know and cannot do will be on display. This is again in contrast to their ordinary working experience, where they demonstrate their competence daily. This slight feeling of apprehension is exacerbated for many participants by associations of training with school, and their dim memories of having 'failed' at school. (Most people do, sadly.)

Training objectives will reduce anxiety by stating straightforwardly the boundaries of training, by making explicit the demands training will place on participants. Usually the reality looks much more manageable and less threatening than participants' vague fears. The participants' annoyance is about somebody being about to 'do something to them'. They feel slightly out of control. Training objectives put them back in control. They can hold the training providers accountable for meeting those objectives.

There is one final and slightly subtle reason why setting objectives for training is such a vital step. It has to do with the training designer's balancing act between the customer's demands and the participants' wishes. The training objectives are the opportunity to show a successful reconciliation between those demands and wishes and a piece of training which has something for everyone.

In this chapter I tell you, step by step, how to get, word, and use objectives for training to achieve all these considerable benefits.

Step one: getting objectives
Whom to ask

I was once asked to design some management skills training for graduate recruits in a high street bank. They would have been in the bank for about four years, and would have had general interpersonal skills training already. They would be coming up to positions of management responsibility, but not in those positions yet.

I asked the customer what the training was intended to achieve. What was happening now which needed to change? What problem should the training resolve for the organisation? He replied that there was nothing specific, that there was a view that people should have management skills training as a preparation for management, and that there was a philosophy in the bank that graduates should have a general developmental training programme every two years.

I declined to design – or indeed deliver – this training. Where there are no real objectives, no changes in skill, knowledge or attitude, which the customer can define, it is not only unlikely the training will be effective but also you will not be able to measure whether it has been effective or not. Participants are likely to feel confused, disappointed, even irritated: some will of course use the training opportunity to achieve objectives of their own, but many will wonder whether they are attending 'Mickey Mouse training' – training for the sake of it, rather than training with urgency and purpose. So, if you cannot get objectives for a piece of training, do not embark on it.

Typically, when you first know of the requirement for a piece of training design, it will be vaguely expressed. 'We must get some more sales skills into these people.' 'We need a course on report writing.' 'A lot of people need more advanced presentation skills.' The training designer needs to turn that vague expression of a requirement into objectives.

Whom should you talk to, to get the objectives? Table 10, opposite, lists all the people you could consult, and the pros and cons of consulting each. When you're deciding how many and who, you need to follow three principles:

- Consult *until* you get purpose, urgency and clarity, until you are confident that there is a real need for the training and that you know what the need is.
- Consult the people who know most about the need.
- Consult the people who should be supporting the training and its outcomes – especially people who are disaffected or hostile but who need to be involved.

> Identify a training requirement you know your organisation has. Imagine you are going to be involved in designing that training. Work through Table 10 with that training requirement in mind, and identify people whom you would consult about the training objectives. Imagine the conversations. What would each person you talked to add to your understanding of the requirement?

Table 10

PEOPLE TO CONSULT ABOUT TRAINING OBJECTIVES, AND THE PROS AND CONS OF CONSULTING THEM

People	Pros	Cons
Customer	▪ his requirement needs to be satisfied: he's paying the bill! ▪ he may have very strong views and a high degree of clarity about what is to be achieved	▪ he may have been asked to organise the training by someone else and not be very clear on what it is to achieve: if so, consult both him and the 'real' customer
Senior/top management	▪ they often have a good overview of what the organisation's needs are ▪ if these people support the training and its outcomes, it is very helpful	▪ they may be too distant from the real issues driving the training ▪ you can't consult them about every single piece of training: you need to prioritise
Internal 'customers' of intended participants (for example, colleagues who need services and co-operation, direct reports)	▪ they may be very close to, and insightful about, the real training needs	▪ their view of what needs to change may be over-influenced by their personal agendas
External customers of intended participants	▪ this type of consultation can build strong relationships between the organisation and its customers ▪ training objectives will be directly linked to commercial drivers ▪ external people can add a unique and insightful perspective	▪ many participants do not have external customers ▪ it may be commercially risky to raise training needs with external customers ▪ customers may simply not know enough about the issues
The participants themselves	▪ this type of consultation can build commitment to the training before it starts ▪ participants are closest of all to the issues	▪ participants may feel they are being 'second-guessed' or manipulated ▪ participants who are not chosen to be consulted may feel disaffected

How to ask them

You can be opportunistic in how you go about consulting people on training objectives, particularly if you belong to the organisation for which you are designing the training. Snatched conversations over lunch and coffee are often the best way of getting the information you need without appearing to be making a mountain out of a molehill every time you are asked to design a piece of training. Also, you will have your own information channels on the corporate grapevine. This is one way in which internal training designers have an edge over external ones.

But a short yet formal series of interviews with a carefully selected series of people can also be a good idea, particularly if the training needs touch on sensitive, confidential or complex issues. Another very rich source of information is a discussion group, where you can listen to the various stakeholders discuss and debate the nature of the 'real problem'. Beware of taking a sledgehammer to crack a nut, though: reserve these more structured approaches for pieces of training design which are:

∎ brand new
∎ a significant investment for the organisation
∎ high potential risk, high potential gain.

What to ask them

As in all investigations, the questions you ask will determine the quality of information you get back. Here are some of the best.

∎ What changes should the training bring about? What should people do differently as a result?
∎ How will you know these changes have occurred? What will you see/hear/ feel differently?
∎ How will the organisation benefit? What will the concrete evidence of those benefits be?

▌ What first made you think this training was necessary?

▌ On a scale of one to ten, where one is the current problematic state of affairs and ten is the ideal state, what degree of improvement would it be acceptable for the training to deliver? Are you looking for a ten? Or will a five do? What would a ten look like? What would a five look like?

▌ Describe the situation 'as is' which needs to change. Now describe the desired situation, the situation 'to be'.

▌ What could happen in this training programme which would make it worthwhile for you?

Step two: wording objectives

When you put the objectives into words, you are marketing the training. You are marketing it to the customer, the participants, and anyone else who has an interest or a stake in it, so marketing principles apply.

▌ Use the language your audience uses. Avoid jargon they do not recognise; use the jargon they are enthusiastic about. In particular, use the words your participants like.

▌ Make the training sound interesting – and fun, if possible. 'To learn how to write reports which people enjoy reading' is a much more engaging objective than 'To learn advanced report-writing skills'.

▌ Make the sentences short, use active rather than passive words; and don't list too many objectives!

Table 11 on page 40 gives some examples of well-worded objectives which confirm to these principles, and poorly worded ones which do not.

Table 11

GOOD AND BAD EXAMPLES OF TRAINING OBJECTIVES

Good examples	Bad examples
∎ to plan to get the best out of this team	∎ to transform this team into a 'high performing team'

(This organisation hated 'psychobabble', and the participants were suspicious of theories and sociological research.)

∎ to give managers more confidence in handling difficult discussions about performance	∎ to ensure performance problems are confronted earlier and more effectively

(The words 'confronted' and 'problems' would immediately make participants feel anxious; the 'bad example' contained a strong, implied criticism of their managerial performance to date.)

∎ to identify organisational barriers to achieving a high level of customer service ∎ to plan to overcome those barriers	∎ to change the organisational culture from task focus to customer focus

(The 'bad' example sounds vague and manipulative, the 'good' one is specific and straightforward.)

∎ to learn the key principles of drawing up a business case ∎ to explore whether and how we can use those principles here	∎ to introduce effective business planning including cost–benefit analyses, risk management, strategic option identification, SWOT and alternative scenario generation

(The 'bad' example looks more like a syllabus than an objective, and it does not allow for participants expressing their views on the relevance of business planning to them.)

Also, some standard objective-setting principles apply, namely, the need for objectives to be 'SMART' – Specific, Measurable, Achievable, Relevant, Time-bound.

Specific   Not 'to improve managers' management skill' but rather 'to practise and get feedback on skills in setting work, reviewing performance, and coaching'.

Measurable   Not 'to upgrade managers' business French' but rather 'to enable participants to conduct a first prospect meeting in French'.

Achievable   Not 'to bring about effective time management in all administrative staff' but rather 'to enable administrative staff to prioritise and delegate more effectively'.

Relevant   Not 'to learn negotiation skills' but rather 'to increase effectiveness in getting supplier costs down'.

Time-bound This is often best ensured by wording the objectives in the format illustrated in Table 12.

Table 12

AN EFFECTIVE WAY TO WORD OBJECTIVES

By the end of this programme, each participant will:

▌ understand the organisational structure

▌ know who is the first point of contact for different types of information

▌ be able to deliver a short presentation on the organisation's mission and values

▌ be able to conduct an induction interview.

> If you can, seek out some examples of training objectives which have been used in your organisation. Test them against the principles in this section. If they are not up to the mark, in your view, edit them until they are.

Step Three: using objectives

There are three key places to use objectives in training design: at the start of the training; in the middle of the training; at the end of the training. Below I give guidelines on how to build them into the design at each of these stages.

Using objectives at the start

■ It is best if participants have seen the objectives before they come on the training. Even so, after introductions, the training objectives should be presented. Many participants will not have read them thoroughly; some will have read them but not fully understood them.

■ You must design in the opportunity for participants to say whether the objectives look reasonable to them. You should also make sure they can add supplementary objectives of their own.

■ You should also design in a brief discussion on 'how will we know if these objectives have been achieved?'

■ Finally, you should ensure there is a commitment to reviewing the training against the objectives at the end.

■ Sometimes a useful approach, particularly if participants are very sceptical about the training's value, is to ask them to estimate their current level of skill or knowledge on the dimensions the training is addressing. By asking them to give themselves a simple numerical rating between one and ten, you uncover issues such as extreme lack of confidence or belief that they don't need training. Then the training deliverer knows what he is working with. Also, he can ask for scores again at the end of the learning, as a measure of its effectiveness. Table 13 illustrates this simple process.

Table 13

GETTING PARTICIPANTS TO SCORE THEMSELVES AGAINST OBJECTIVES

Objective of training: to improve participants' skills in conducting effective appraisal discussions

1   Present objective. Ask participants: 'Does it look reasonable? What sort of changes would you consider evidence of improvement?'

2   Ask participants to answer the following question by giving themselves a score between one and ten. 'How confident do you feel in your ability to conduct an effective appraisal discussion?'

3   Discuss any extreme scores with participants. Commit to reviewing scores at the end of the training.

Using objectives in the middle

■ About half-way through a training intervention, you should design in a fairly formal check with the participants that it is working for them.

■ The most straightforward way to do this is to remind them of the objectives, and ask them – for each objective – what the benefits have been so far of the training and what their remaining concerns are. Table 14 on page 44 illustrates the kind of information you should get.

■ The training design will of course have to allow for modifications in response to concerns raised (see Chapter 5, pages 64–66 'Manoeuvrability').

Using objectives at the end

■ By designing in a review of progress against objectives at the end, you not only provide an immediate measure

Table 14

EXAMPLE OUTPUT OF A MID-PROGRAMME REVIEW AGAINST OBJECTIVES

Objective: to practise, get feedback on, and improve presentation skills

Benefits	Concerns
■ saw myself on video – learned a lot about nonverbals	■ I wish I knew how to deal with awkward questions
■ got audience reaction to my style	■ I need more practice with the OHP
■ did three short presentations, with feedback	■ I'm still anxious about giving long presentations

of training effectiveness. You also demonstrate that the training was designed and delivered with commitment, with a willingness to be held accountable.

■ Sometimes it is best to conduct this review as a discussion, and sometimes best for individual questionnaires to be handed out. It depends on whether the group will be too tired or too focused on other things at the end of the training to engage in yet another group activity. The training designer should provide both options, and let the deliverer judge which is best at the time.

Overt objectives and hidden agendas

I have already pointed out that objectives are a piece of marketing as well as a statement of what is to be expected. So clearly there are often aspects to the training requirement which are not stated overtly in the objectives. Imagine how difficult it would be to learn anything useful once you had been introduced to a piece of training in any of the following terms:

■ to change your attitude from an individualistic one to a team-playing one

▌ to prevent you upsetting people in the way you conduct appraisals

▌ to convince you the new sales process is better then the old one.

Such objectives focus unhelpfully on criticisms of the current state of the participants, and sound deterministic, aggressive even. They are totally inappropriate.

This is not just a point about marketing, however. If the training designer starts work believing it is the job of training to force or manipulate people into different ways of behaving, the training is likely to fail. But more than that, this attitude is operating against the real spirit of training, in my view. For training is about releasing people's creativity and potential in the right direction, not about containing and controlling it.

So as a training designer you should work with those who are commissioning the training until you can agree an open agenda for the training which translates into the kind of objectives which encourage learning and exploration rather than resistance and defensiveness. You may need to argue quite persistently in some cases against a highly 'political' agenda. If you allow training to turn into propaganda once, all further training from the same source will be compromised.

I have worked on many pieces of training design where the organisation was desperate for its senior managers to buy into a new way of doing things. The training requirement was initially expressed in very controlling terms. 'To get senior managers to be more commercially minded.' 'To ensure everyone does appraisals with all direct reports at least once a year.' In every case, I worked with my customers to refine the requirement into something more appealing to the participants, and also more achievable. 'To explore where commercial approaches can benefit our organisation.' 'To present the benefits of annual appraisal, and give senior managers confidence in their ability to conduct them effectively.' I believe that these kinds of objectives are also more likely to bring about lasting behaviour change of the kind the organisation is seeking – where that is possible.

These arguments about objective-setting are not superficial ones about presentation. They go to the heart of the training designer's values. They are fundamental to designing – and delivering – training which has integrity.

In brief

- Setting objectives is the single most important step in designing training. It focuses the designer's mind. It is the basis for the contract between training designer and customer. And it is the key to winning the participants' commitment.

- To get the basic information you need to set objectives, talk to one or more of the following categories of people: customer(s), senior/top management, colleagues and subordinates of participants, external customers of participants, participants themselves.

- Ask them to define precisely what should change as a result of the training.

- To word objectives effectively, remember they are a piece of marketing for the training. They should be in language the participant recognises and likes. They should be specific, measurable, achievable, relevant, and time-bound.

- Objectives are used to introduce a programme, to review it mid-way, and to review it at the end.

- In honest training – which is effective training – the stated objectives are the real objectives. Training designers should resist the invitation to design propaganda.

The Politics of Training

Introduction

You can achieve as much by the effective positioning of a training intervention in its organisation as by the elegant and appropriate design of content. Positioning training effectively is the politics of training. Effective positioning is achieved to some extent through the objective-setting process, which we looked at in the previous chapter. But two further key questions need to be addressed by training designers before they can be happy that they have got the most out of the politics:

∎ Who should have a say?
∎ What groupings should people be trained in?

It is these two questions to which we now turn our attention.

Who should have a say?

In the previous chapter we looked at who should have a say in setting objectives. There are two categories of people who should have a say, whether or not they are included in the objective-setting process. They are:

∎ People who can block.
∎ People who can contribute.

Let's think about training 'blockers' first.

Training blockers

On only very rare occasions can organisations organise training for all of their people simultaneously. (Some big company values programmes 'hit' everyone almost simultaneously, but this is the exception.) So generally people return from training to a working environment where there are many people who haven't been on that particular training programme and who are not prepared to expect – or even accept – any kind of behaviour change, and may act in ways which prevent it. Then the value of the training for those who attended it is lost.

Let me give you an example. A pharmaceuticals company made a considerable investment in an analytical trouble-shooting problem-solving course for first-line supervisors. They became skilled in the problem-solving process, and enthusiastic about its application to the sorts of production problems they encountered daily. They felt it had the potential to cut 'down-time' (that is, time when production was interrupted) considerably.

But when they returned to the workplace, they discovered that the groups which needed to solve the production problems contained a minority of people who had been trained. The others saw the formal problem-solving process as unnecessary and cumbersome: after all, they had not been exposed to its benefits on the training programme. It was impossible for the first-line supervisors to impose the process, particularly in groups where they were not the boss. They became disheartened, gave up trying to use the technique, and ultimately forgot it.

What could have been done differently to position this training intervention more effectively? Here are just three suggestions:

▮ A questionnaire survey with all the workforce could have been carried out on production problems and down-time prior to the course being run. The course could then have been presented as a partial solution to a problem everyone had contributed to identifying.

People would have been expecting a change in general working practices when first-line supervisors came back from the training – maybe even looking forward to it!

■ All bosses of first-line supervisors could have been briefed on the programme and on their part in supporting first-line supervisors in making use of what they had learned.

■ People could have attended the programme in real problem-solving work groups, so that a whole team would learn to use the technique together.

(The final point is, of course, about the groupings in which people should be trained. This aspect of the politics of training is so important I shall discuss it further shortly.)

You might think 'what a palaver' when you read the ideas of what could have been done differently. 'All the organisation wanted was to introduce some simple problem-solving techniques quickly. Does it really have to jump through all these hoops?'

The answer is 'yes'. When training interventions fail to produce long-lasting benefits in the workplace, it is usually because they have not been properly positioned. Hardly any organisation does enough to position training, even nowadays when everyone is talking the language of 'business-driven HR'.

If you as the training designer do not anticipate the organisational training blockers and act to defuse their destructive potential in advance, you can design the 'best' programme ever and it will have only a fraction of the impact it could.

Here is a quick summary of the steps you can take to defuse blockers – and turn them into contributors:

■ Use the grapevine to spread understanding and expectations of a training intervention.

■ Ask participants to talk to their colleagues, boss and others around them before and after they come on the programme; ask them to find out 'what's in it for my colleagues?'

- Brief bosses.
- Interview and/or survey blockers ostensibly to get information relevant to training design.
- Invite blockers to all or part of the training.
- Include in blockers' own training elements designed to help and encourage them to support colleagues' training outcomes.
- Make sure that during training participants think about and plan for the reactions they will get when they return to the workplace.

I would say for every hour you spend planning content, you should spend at least two positioning the intervention.

Potential contributors

We focused on training blockers first. In fact, people who can contribute to the training's design and effectiveness are often exactly the same people as the so-called blockers. For they are by definition people who are close to the training outcomes. But there are some other potential contributors you should not forget:

- people who have designed or delivered (or both) training to your participants before
- people who have designed or delivered (or both) this type of training in this organisation before
- people who have attended this type of training before
- people in the organisation with vision and breadth of thinking.

What groupings should people be trained in?

It is amazing to me how much training still happens in 'horizontal slices'. (By 'horizontal slice' I mean groups of people all at the same level in an organisation – for example, graduate recruits, directors, or operators.) There are so many other possibilities, offering the training designer so much scope for effective positioning. We have seen one of those possibilities already, and its potential to defuse or diminish training blocks (see page 49).

So let us consider a whole variety of approaches to training groupings and the pros and cons of each. That way, you will at least be aware of the choices, even if convention still pushes you down the 'horizontal slice' track nine times out of ten.

Cascade

In the cascade approach, you start at the top and work down. So, for example, if you were designing appraisal skills training, you might design it to be delivered first to the MD and his or her team, then to all directors, then to directors' first reports, and so on, until all those with managerial responsibility had been covered.

Pros

■ This approach is particularly effective when the behaviours on which training is focused are ones people would expect their bosses to set a good example in. Appraisal skills is one such type of training; presentation skills, selling skills, word-processing skills, for example, may not be. (It is because of this 'pro' that the cascade approach is often the best choice for major culture change interventions.)

■ Bosses are more likely to support training outcomes for their subordinates if they have been trained themselves. If a manager, for example, is setting aside a substantial amount of time to conduct appraisals, their boss is less likely to put pressure on him to cancel appraisal interviews for operational reasons if he or she has been trained in the importance of high quality appraisal.

■ You can effectively pilot a new programme with more

senior people, and use their comments to improve and refine it.

∎ If people have seen their bosses attend a training programme first, the credibility of the programme is increased.

Cons

∎ On the whole, in the USA and Europe, the more senior that people are, the less time they invest in their own development. So the more senior people will certainly be unwilling to head up a cascade for too many training interventions.

∎ Often the more senior people are under more urgent operational pressure. If the whole intervention depends on their doing it first, it may be unacceptably delayed.

∎ Of course, much training is for subgroups only. Then a whole organisation cascade would be totally inappropriate; a mini-cascade down two or three levels or in one department only might be appropriate, but certainly not in every case.

One particularly effective cascade occurred in a furniture manufacturer and retailer. First of all, the 'top team' participated in workshops to discuss and define the company's values, and the new behaviours which should result from these. Particular importance was placed on customer service, both internal and external. The workshops were then cascaded throughout the whole organisation, with each level adding new insight to the values and behaviours framework. The effectiveness of the cascade lay in the actions which participants committed to during each workshop: people saw their bosses behaving differently and, indeed, treating them better, before they went on the workshop and that made them very enthusiastic about the process, willing to take on actions themselves.

Workgroups

On the basis of my experience of designing and delivering training, I would say the workgroup approach was the single most under-utilised approach, given its potential benefits. Ask yourself, for every piece of training you design, 'Would the workgroup approach be a good one here?' It is not, of course, universally appropriate, but it could be used far more, to good effect.

Pros

■ Transfer of learning to the workplace is much more likely, because people are learning and changing with their colleagues. The whole jigsaw is changing simultaneously, as opposed to just one or two pieces on their own.

■ Colleagues will support and challenge each other after the training.

■ The workgroup can bring real and relevant issues to the training room to be dealt with. In the analytical trouble-shooting problem-solving course referred to earlier in this chapter (see page 48), workgroups could have tried the techniques out on their most important and pressing current problems.

■ The leader will be learning with his team, and will be more inclined to support training outcomes later.

■ There is a general teambuilding benefit on even the most non-teambuilding training programmes. For example, I was once running a report-writing course for a workgroup in an engineering company. Not only were a lot of team issues sorted out over lunch and breaks, but the participants decided on a set of report-writing standards which they would adopt as a team after the course. Imagine how unlikely that outcome would have been if only one or two members from that workgroup had attended.

Think about your own workgroup – your boss, immediate colleagues, people who work for you. Imagine that group attending together a variety of training programmes. You might like to think about, for example, appraisal and appraisee skills training, IT training, a managing change programme and a personal development programme. (Such training is usually *not* delivered to workgroups.) What specific spin-off benefits could your workgroup gain from such experiences? Is there a rumbling conflict which could be resolved? Are there ideas for improving working habits which would come out of discussions?

Cons

■ If a whole workgroup goes away on a training programme together, it may cause operational problems.

■ If the training is very challenging, members of the same workgroup may be reluctant to experiment, expose themselves, and possibly fail in front of each other. A related point is that for some types of training the leader may want to learn 'in private'. Interestingly, I have often found this to be very important when designing team leader training: whilst team leaders want teambuilding in their teams, they often also want some leadership skills training with other leaders.

■ If relationships in the workgroup are either fraught or too 'chummy', they can get in the way of learning.

Horizontal slices

Of course there are some good reasons for choosing to deliver training to groups of people who have little in common apart from being currently at the same hierarchical position in an organisation. You just need to be sure you have chosen this for one or more of the good reasons below, and not just *faute de mieux*.

Pros

▪ Many types of training are most appropriate at a particular hierarchical level. Examples would be introductory management skills for first line managers, strategic management skills for directors, project management skills for ... project managers! This is the best reason for delivering training in horizontal slices.

▪ Particularly for the type of training just described, the horizontal slices approach offers the important auxiliary benefit of networking across that particular hierarchical level. This means ideas can be exchanged, problems shared, and common concerns discussed, either as part of the training proper or in breaks. Participants will have a lot in common from the point of view of their daily activities and responsibilities at work.

▪ Logistically, the horizontal slices approach has appeal. The course can be advertised as for a particular level, then simply left for people to arrange cover and apply. It is not a heavy administrative burden on the training department, nor a heavy operational burden, providing not too many people at a single level are being trained simultaneously. This approach does not require complicated planning of who attends with whom, as can the cascade and workgroup approaches.

Surprisingly, I have seen a 'thick horizontal slice' approach work well in a culture change programme. The top four levels of management in an international charity attended a five-day residential workshop in groups of twenty. Participants were selected so that each programme was itself truly international, and so rare and important networking across and also up and down a section of the organisation was achieved. I think the programme worked well (in terms of long-lasting effectiveness) because the slices were so thick, and in fact represented 20 to 30 per cent of the organisation. It also worked well because the groupings were chosen so as to break down vertical barriers between different countries and different departments. (The only problem was that people just below the first level eligible felt rather aggrieved at being excluded.)

Cons

- The main disadvantage to the horizontal slice approach is that participants are highly likely to return to a daily working environment where they are the only person who's had the training. As we have already discussed, this means lasting change is much less likely.

- Training is a great opportunity to break down long-standing organisational barriers. (See 'Pros' above.) The horizontal slice approach often does not make the most of this opportunity, since some of the most destructive barriers tend to be hierarchical ones, which are only reinforced by the approach.

- If participants think they are going on a course simply because 'everyone at this level does it', they are less likely to be curious about the course, and less likely to learn from it.

'Sheep dip'

This is training delivered to a lot of people, in randomly determined groupings. As the nickname implies, it is an unintelligent approach to delivery, likely to make participants feel herded into an experience of no particular relevance to them. It usually happens when organisations do not have the expertise or the will to think carefully about the positioning of a training intervention, and/or when the people positioning the training don't know very much about the population for whom the training is being provided. This is 'lack of intelligence' in more than one sense.

The amount of sheep-dipping which still goes on is quite staggering. Just to cite one example, a fairly small organisation (which should have had the time and resources to know better) recently sent all its professional staff details of the training for which they had to sign up over the next twelve months. Everyone had been put down for a two-day 'customer care' workshop, a half-day 'telephone skills' seminar, and a three-day residential programme on 'personal and professional development'.

The very fact that this menu had been applied to everyone undermined its credibility, and soon individual objections started circulating; such as that from one member of staff who had no telephone but had still been put down for telephone skills; and from the person who had only six months previously completed a module on 'personal and professional development' as part of her Open University course.

Such unintelligent positioning of training deserves only unintelligent responses from the participants. And that precludes learning.

Vertical slices

This is training for operational subgroups in an organisation. Similar pros and cons as for horizontal slices apply, although it can be more exciting to take a vertical slice approach because it does potentially break the hierarchical barriers. An example would be a customer service programme for *everyone* in a finance department. Examples of appropriate vertical slice training would be Business French for the marketing department (specifically focused on relevant vocabulary and situations) and systems design principles for the IT department.

Cellular

A lot of training is in fact delivered to organisational 'cells' – that is, small groups defined both horizontally and vertically. Examples would be Selling Skills for sales managers in the marketing department, Systems Design Principles for senior IT managers, and Business French for negotiators in the contracts department. Where the content of the training means it really is only applicable to a 'cell', then this approach is inevitable. Otherwise, the training designer should always try either to break down destructive organisational barriers or to build the effectiveness of real work groups in designing the groupings for his or her interventions.

In brief

■ Positioning training appropriately in an organisation is as important as designing good content.

■ The two key questions in positioning training are:

  ◻ who should have a say in training design

  ◻ what groups should people be trained in?

■ People who may block training by being unhelpful, unsupportive or sceptical towards participants when they return from training should have a say. Then they are less likely to block.

■ Also, potential 'blockers' may have a lot to contribute. Participants' colleagues, bosses and subordinates can be blockers or contributors. By the right kind of consultation, the training designer can transform them from the first into the second.

■ The main choices in deciding what groupings people should be trained in are:

  ◻ cascade

  ◻ workgroups

  ◻ horizontal slices

  ◻ vertical slices

  ◻ cellular

  ◻ sheep-dip.

■ The majority of training is delivered is horizontal slices, cellular or sheep-dip groups. Yet the other approaches have much to recommend them, and should be used more.

■ Each approach to groupings has advantages and disadvantages, and is most appropriate to certain types of training. The training designer should make a conscious and intelligent choice, bearing in mind two key principles:

☐ try to use training as an opportunity to break down destructive organisational barriers, and build effective co-operation

☐ choose from the appropriate approaches to grouping the one which will help behaviour change to transfer to, and last in, the daily work environment.

5

The Key Dimensions of Training Design

Introduction

Every piece of training design is unique. By the time you have imagined your audience (in and outside the training room), fully understood the objectives, and investigated the politics, you will see each design challenge as a new one. In fact, for the training designer, adopting a 'standard approach' is a sure sign of impending disaster.

So, you may ask, if every piece of training design is unique, how can I learn the trade? What pre-set structures will help me in the early stages? How can I use my growing experience as a designer of training to become more skilful?

The key to this lies in five aspects of training which should be in every training designer's mind, constantly. He or she should be looking for ways to address these aspects in every element of the training, mentally testing the design against the demands these aspects make and using experience of training which works and training which does not to identify design approaches which address these aspects increasingly effectively. In this chapter we present and discuss them: the key concepts of training design. We then provide 10 fundamental design principles linked to the key concepts, to ensure the training you design is set for success right from the start. So, by the end of this chapter you will know how to think about training to design it well. You will also have a set of practical guidelines for putting your thinking to good effect.

Five key concepts
Credibility

In Chapter 1, we identified the 'special' nature of training. People take time off 'normal work' to do it. In Chapter 4, we began to explore the difficulties in transfer of learning to the workplace. So we come to the concept of credibility, which is at the heart of designing training.

Training has to prove its relevance, because on the whole it is apart from work. And the reason much training has little effect on behaviour at work is that, quite simply, the participants don't believe in it. They do not believe it is relevant, they do not believe it is important, they do not believe it is an effective use of their time.

So training designers must ask themselves at every stage: what can I do to increase the credibility of this training intervention? Otherwise their training will meet with cynical rejection.

Commitment

This concept is linked to credibility, because if participants believe in a training intervention then they are more likely to commit to it. But it deserves separate consideration, because it is about much more than belief.

It is about investment. The more each participant invests personally in a programme, the more effect it will have. It's rather like the old argument that the more you pay for something the more you're likely to value it.

Let me give you an example, in the training context. Imagine a training intervention on the topic of leadership skills. One such intervention might require the participants to listen to seminars, hold discussions, solve real life leadership problems together, and draw up action plans. Another might require each participant to take a turn at leading the group in a challenging task: staging a play to be videoed, for example, or making a presentation to a senior and highly critical manager. Let us assume both interventions have equal credibility. Participants believe they are relevant, important, and effective. But they are still very different on the dimension of commitment.

The seminar/discussion/problem-solving intervention requires commitment of time, effort and creativity. But the practical leadership intervention requires each participant to put their own performance on the line in a highly exposed way. Participants must invest much more.

Often it is not appropriate to ask participants to invest so much. But the training designer must look for opportunities throughout the intervention to gain more commitment from the participants. To get them to 'put their money where their mouth is'. Or the training will flow over them, like water off a duck's back.

Unless the training designer elicits significant commitment from each participant, there is a risk that they will sit back and mentally say, 'This is all well and good. But, basically, it's for somebody else.'

Risk

To get commitment, you have to get people to take risks. But you must manage that risk: you must make sure the degree of risk you expect your participants to take is proportional to the degree of benefit they can expect to get in return, and appropriate to their emotional state.

For example, do not expect people to take high risks at the start of a programme. They are probably already uneasy, have established no relationship yet with the tutors, and may well be wary of each other. If you open a programme with a session in which each individual has to relate, for example, their biggest professional mistake as a manager, you are very likely to encounter frightened rejection. Yet I have seen that very session work well after dinner three days into a residential programme, in which people have been giving feedback, coaching one another, and discussing differences in management style. They were ready for the risk, by then.

If you design no- or very low-risk training programmes, no or low impact will be the result. If you throw high-risk interventions at people with no lead-in, or lead-out, participants will, quite simply, walk away from the training.

Here is an illustration from a classic teambuilding intervention. One of the most high-risk and (therefore) potentially effective elements of such an intervention comprises each team member giving each of the other team members two pieces of honest feedback, one positive, one negative. Typically, they will be asked to complete the following two sentences for each of their colleagues:

> 'You make an effective contribution as a member of this team because...'

> 'Your contribution would be more effective if you...'

If you design this element in at the start of the teambuilding intervention, people are likely to fudge it. They will complete the sentences dishonestly or blandly. You have not managed the risk of exposure for them; so they are managing it for themselves. They are, effectively, walking away from your intervention, and it will be hard work to bring them back. In training, as in life, their own survival is their top priority.

If you design this element in after they have spent some time together comfortably, shared some successes with tasks, made minor forays into feedback with no ill effects, and got to the point where they want, at last, to sort out some team issues which have been hampering their work for some time, then they will engage. They will be careful about what they say, and nervous about receiving the feedback – but I have met people who have remembered a session like this, and the message it contained, decades later.

The training designer must question at all stages of design: have I managed the risk to which participants are exposed, have I used it as a tool to bring about change whilst ensuring I have not used it thoughtlessly or unrealistically?

Attention

People's level of attention fluctuates. Unless positive steps are taken to engage attention repeatedly, it declines. It declines when people are passive – listening or watching without action. It declines when people are bored. It declines when they know what is coming, and that what is coming is not interesting.

The training designer needs to approach his task as a fight against the decline of attention. However fascinated the designer is in the content of the training – and he probably will be, that is one of the reasons he has got the job – he should never assume fascination on the part of the participants. If anything, he should assume boredom.

> At the next meeting or presentation you go to, study your own pattern of paying attention. When are you most attentive? What causes your attention (or you!) to drop off? What makes you prick up your ears? Who is the best speaker you know, in terms of holding your attention? What makes them good?

Manoeuvrability

The training designer and the training deliverer are a partnership, even when they don't know each other. Of course, they are often one and the same, and that is ideal (see Chapter 2, page 25 for why). But even when they are not, the success of an intervention depends on both their efforts, and it depends at least as much on the deliverer's skill in making the training work as it does on the designer's skill in putting it together in the first place.

The training designer needs to capitalise on the maybe as yet unseen partner to make the training work. The training deliverer needs to be allowed the space and opportunity to adapt the programme to the group, to the atmosphere, to events which occur unexpectedly in and outside the training room. The course needs to be designed for manoeuvrability.

On a simple level, elements need to be designed that can work with different sizes of group. If the design is totally dependent on participants working in trios, what can the deliverer do when one of the participants falls ill and there are 11 on the course instead of 12?

On a more sophisticated level, elements need to be designed that allow the deliverer scope to engage attention more directly and to manage risk.

Two examples will perhaps clarify this. The first focuses on the issue of attention. I was delivering an interpersonal skills programme to a mixed group of American and British managers. The Americans' flight had been delayed. By the afternoon of the first day, I could see that jet lag had set in: the Americans' eyes were literally closing. The training had been designed around a large group discussion of the difference between managers and leaders in the early afternoon. But the programme was flexible enough for me to split people into much smaller groups and give them some interesting management problems to act out and solve instead. This kept them awake until the go-karting session at 4 o'clock!

The second example focuses on risk. I was once delivering an appraisal skills course to a group of middle managers. They were called out for a company announcement at lunch time on the second day of a three-day programme. The announcement concerned large-scale redundancies, the detail of which would be announced in a week's time. When the managers came back, they were so anxious that it was no time to share openly the results of questionnaires their subordinates had completed on their appraisal skills. Their external environment had suddenly become so high-risk, the training environment needed to be made much safer. Fortunately, the planned session could be run without anyone disclosing their results.

If you do not design for manoeuvrability, you are failing to exploit your biggest asset: the deliverer.

Ten fundamental design principles

The key concepts of credibility, commitment, risk, attention and manoeuvrability lead to some absolutely fundamental principles of good training design. I shall now describe these principles in theory and in practice. Table 15 opposite shows how following each of the design principles contributes to meeting the requirements dictated by the five key concepts. If you follow all these principles, you can be sure that the training you design will:

∎ establish its credibility
∎ elicit the participants' commitment
∎ manage risk
∎ attract attention
∎ allow manoeuvrability.

Maximise action and interaction

This is, of course, the classic way to help people keep paying attention. Even in a lecture context, the teacher who is really interested in being listened to will ask rhetorical questions, pause before he gives the answer to a problem he has posed, and include opportunities for brief discussion between himself and his audience, and between members of the audience. He knows that the longer people are required to be passive recipients, the more likely it is that their minds will wander.

How much more relevant this principle is to training. For in training, remember, we are dealing primarily with behaviour change not knowledge transfer. New behaviour is learned by people trying it out, not on the whole by listening to others describe it. So by maximising action and interaction, the training designer not only engages

Table 15

THE 10 FUNDAMENTAL DESIGN PRINCIPLES' IMPACT

Key concepts

Design principles	Credibility	Commitment	Risk	Attention	Manoeuvrability
1 Maximise action and interaction		✓	✓	✓	
2 Signpost, signpost, and then signpost again	✓	✓	✓	✓	
3 Vary pace and rhythm				✓	
4 Chunk content				✓	✓
5 Map the participants' world	✓	✓		✓	
6 Give participants choices		✓	✓		✓
7 Surface objections		✓	✓	✓	✓
8 Balance theory and practice	✓			✓	
9 Design in feedback		✓	✓		
10 Design for closure		✓		✓	

and keeps people's attention, but also builds their commitment to new behaviour – because they have tried it out for themselves, rather than left it sitting abstract on some shelf – and creates opportunities for people to risk success or failure and so increase the impact of their learning. In Table 16 on page 68, I give some examples of how to maximise action and interaction for training elements.

Table 16

TRANSFORMING TRAINING ELEMENTS

Non-interactive ('unreconstructed') elements →	Elements for action and interaction
Presentation of course objectives using OHP.	Invitation to course participants to brainstorm possible objectives of course; link these to predetermined objectives and amend the predetermined ones.
Short lecture on the nature of 'mission' in organisations.	Divide people into groups; ask them to identify two organisations that seem to them to have a strong 'mission'; ask them what it is that makes them seem that way; discuss it and how these characteristics could apply to their own organisation.
Presentation of the principles of good quality feedback.	Divide the group into trios: person A is asked to give feedback to person B on a task he or she did earlier. Person C gives person A feedback on his or her feedback. (And so on!)

I am sure you will have realised that one of the main reasons for the very common training approach of dividing participants into syndicates or 'break out' groups to discuss issues is precisely to maximise action and interaction. The problem is that sometimes training designers and deliverers forget that syndicates are a means to that end and not an end in themselves. They neglect to give the syndicates varied and interesting tasks, and allow the 'big group/ syndicate work/presentations back to the group' format to become sterile and repetitive.

Turning passive elements into active and interactive ones rapidly becomes a creative habit for the good training designer who will see opportunities to do so in surprising places. I was particularly impressed by a piece of training designed by an image consultant. It was active and interactive from the start. She even made her personal introduction active and interactive by asking the participants to guess facts about her! (She then used their mistakes to illustrate the power of dress and personal presentation to mislead others about your background, character, and abilities.)

Signpost, signpost and then signpost again

The training designer knows, by definition, what each step in a training programme is there for, how it contributes to the whole, why it is necessary to achieve the training objectives. After you have been working on a piece of training design for even a short time, you are so close to it, so immersed in it, that its content seems totally logical to you, the reasoning behind it transparent. After all, it is your reasoning.

But that is not how it will seem to your participants. There they are, for the most part, like fish out of water. It is often not clear to them even why they are in the training room in the first place, let alone why you have just asked them to introduce themselves to the group. And now, even though you surely know that their presentation skills are not very good (after all, this is a presentation skills course), you are asking them to be videoed giving a two-minute talk on 'something which annoys them'. Why aren't you teaching them something first? And, being human, they will, in the absence of explanation from you, be inventing explanations of their own. Such as, that you want to embarrass them at the start of the programme so that they will pay more attention.

In fact, when you designed this start to the training course, your intentions were quite other. You wanted each participant to build on his natural presentation style, and wanted to help him diagnose his natural strengths using the video. In fact, according to the good principle of agreeing objectives clearly at the beginning of the programme, you had included a bullet point in the second overhead stating: 'You will learn how to capitalise on natural presentation abilities as observed on video.'

These kinds of misunderstandings between the training designer and the participants in the training are very destructive to the training objectives. They can lead to:

- loss of credibility, because the participants simply do not understand the point of what they are being asked to do
- lack of commitment, because the participants do not see the relevance to them as individuals
- poorly managed risk, with participants too confused to take risk, or thinking that they are taking more risk than they are (as in the presentation skills example)
- and lapses of attention, as participants turn to thinking about things they do understand.

The only way to avoid such misunderstandings is to get into the habit of 'signposting' at every point of the training journey. By signposting, I mean stating explicitly why each training element has been included – and then checking the participants have read the signpost. In the presentation skills example, participants should not only have been given the general information about the use of video. That signpost would have been easily missed in the rush of objective-setting traffic. They should also have been told just before the videoing began exactly what use would be made of the tapes, with a signpost like this:

> You will study your own video, and identify all the positive features of your presentation style, using a checklist the tutor will give you. She will help you do this. Later sessions will be based around helping you to make the most of the positive features you identified.

Video is so anxiety-provoking for many people that there should probably be a further signpost at the end of this training element, repeating why it was done and what it will be used for.

Without adequate signposting, your training programmes will at best confuse participants, at worst enrage them.

You need to cultivate the habit of 'always giving a reason for the hope that is within you'.

Vary pace and rhythm

A training programme is an experience. Like any experience – and the most obvious example is a musical one – it will have more impact if it has variety. Pace and rhythm are key concepts here, and the training designer needs to play an interesting tune with them to keep participants' attention.

Slow pace activities include small group discussions, reflective input to the large group by tutors, reading, completing questionnaires, watching a film, practising certain kinds of skill. The individual participant is not rushed, has time to think, may take 'time out' to think about something else briefly.

Fast pace activities include a high energy input from the tutor with jokes, questions fired, and sparky interaction from and between group members, delivering a product (such as a short play, or a presentation) under tight time pressure, a well-facilitated brainstorming session. The individual participant is busy, very alert, fully occupied.

Good training design will use pace intelligently. Slow and fast pace activities will alternate, allowing for the different kinds of learning which occur.

Variations will also be played on rhythm. One morning may be spent in a succession of short fast pace activities. The afternoon may alternate slow and fast. The next morning may be a whole morning devoted to a slow-pace activity, such as drawing up a personal development plan.

Variety is the training designer's friend. At all costs, avoid a standardised repetitive format. ('It's after break, it must be presentation time.') Imagine experiencing your own training. Are there elements of surprise? Are you out of breath at one point, relaxed at another? If so, you'll probably be paying attention throughout.

Chunk content

Politicians learn to speak in 'sound-bites'. We training designers have to learn to design in 'learning-bites'.

People's attention typically rises at the beginning and end of things, and wanes in the middle. By chunking the content of training, you introduce lots of beginnings and ends, and so increase attention. For example, if you were designing a training programme on report writing, you might chunk it like this:

- how to plan a report (input)
- exercise on planning
- conventions of language (input)
- exercise on good and bad use of language in reports
- critiquing examples of good reports
- the executive summary (input)
- exercise on writing executive summaries
- some tricks of the trade
- lessons from copywriting (guest speaker)
- humour and wit in report writing: interactive video session
- writing reports for each other
- feedback
- plenary discussion on 'how I will write reports differently now'.

Immediately the participants see the menu, the course looks more digestible than it did as an undifferentiated day on 'report writing'. Not only can they see the stages of learning – which makes the learning look more possible – but they can also see variety in the way the chunks are to be tackled. Once the training starts, the pattern of attention rise and fall will be managed by the chunks beginning and ending.

Finally, the chunks give the training deliverer much of the manoeuvrability needed. Suppose participants are concerned right from the start that the organisation is trying to eliminate their individuality by sending them on a standardised report-writing course. The training deliverer can move the session on 'humour and wit' forwards, let them play with some original and creative approaches, put their dominant concern to rest so that they will get more out of the more formal sessions. Or if they seem a very pragmatic bunch, who want quick pay-offs, concrete evidence early that the course is useful, the training deliverer can do the 'some tricks of the trade' session near the beginning.

Map the participants' world

This design principle is all about making the training feel, to each participant, less as if it is 'happening on another planet'. It begins with the objective-setting process (see Chapter 3), and continues with the language of the course, the examples used in the course to illustrate points, and the exercises and tasks the participants are given to practise their skills and explore their application. It is in some ways the most important principle of all and is at the heart of many successful techniques for bringing about behaviour change. It is central to that school of human influence and change known as 'Neurolinguistic Programming', for example, where it is known as 'pacing'. This word is rather an apposite one. It brings to mind the picture of a late passenger trying to jump on a moving train. Think of the passenger jumping as the trainer, the train as the participants. In order to jump on successfully, the passenger has to run alongside the train at the same speed it is moving, matching his speed to the speed of the train, 'pacing' it.

So it is with training. In order to influence participants, you must first show you have understood their world. You must bring your speed up, or down, to theirs. Otherwise you will miss them.

Let me give you a concrete example. A colleague and I were designing a self-development programme for experienced and successful partners in one of the UK's biggest legal firms. In their world, their primary concerns were to do with the extreme pressures their success brought, resulting in lack of time with their families, and with their desire to become still more successful while improving their quality of life. In their world, high charges for high quality service were what they had built their success on, and the firm's 'branding' (brand name, image, reputation) was key to that. In their world, relationships were central to success, although profit was the goal on which their minds were ultimately fixed. Here are some of the steps we took to map their world.

■ We called the programme 'Leading Relationships'. (This also mapped on to a high-profile, firm-wide initiative called 'The Leadership Project'.)

■ We made sure the programme itself had high quality branding (expensive and professional pre-programme publicity, top quality materials, tutors known as the best in their fields).

■ We sold the programme as being about working smarter, not harder, about getting more success for less effort. We made sure that on the programme people worked from 9.00am to 6.00pm, and no longer. We modelled the kind of lifestyle to which they aspired in the timetable for the programme.

■ We built the skills exercises around situations in which relationships had to be built in order to achieve commercial goals. We initiated their exploration of their own strengths and development needs from that starting-point.

Imagine how differently a self-development programme for a group of senior engineers would be. Their watchwords might be technical excellence, intellect, research and evidence. We would include results from studies; quantitative ways of assessing competence, job satisfaction and stress; exercises built round technical challenges.

The end-point of both programmes would be to help each individual establish their own priorities for personal development. The routes to that end-point have to be very different – because the participants come from different worlds.

If you do not map their worlds, they will not believe in the programme ('How can someone who doesn't understand where I'm coming from teach me anything useful?'), they will not engage on a personal level ('this programme must have been written for someone else'), and they will get bored – because their strongest interests have not been accounted for in the content.

Give participants choices

By giving participants choices, you also give the deliverer choices, and more manoeuvrability. But more importantly than that, you increase commitment because the participants see that they are being treated as adults and colleagues. Also, you can design in optional high-risk elements, so that participants can do what they feel ready for. (For example, if you are designing a session on 'managing your boss', you can design it so that people choose whether to talk openly about their boss in response to a series of questions, or simply think the answers.)

What kinds of choices are we talking about? Here are some of the most useful:

- whether to work alone, in pairs, or in groups
- whether to ask for feedback from the tutor
- whether to volunteer to do something in front of the group
- whether to share information, or work on it privately
- whether to be the actor or the observer in a skills exercise
- with whom in the group to work.

As a training designer, you should be looking for every opportunity to give participants choice.

Surface objections

It is well known that for every criticism someone gives voice to, there are at least ten criticisms he keeps to himself. It is the job of both the training designer and the training deliverer to structure the programme so that criticisms are aired – or in the words of the trade, 'objections are surfaced'.

You may wonder, why go looking for trouble? The answer is that when participants have objections (about the quality or relevance of part of the programme, for example), they begin to lose commitment. Then their attention wanders, and you have lost them. So make sure that throughout the programme:

■ reviews are built in: 'What's working well for you? what needs to be different?'

■ formal opportunities to play 'devil's advocate' are built in: for example, on an appraisal skills course, include a session on 'what are the disadvantages of appraisal?'

■ checks are built in: less extensive than reviews, these are questions at the end of every training element such as 'was that useful?', 'how relevant was that to the work situation?'

By doing this, you also make sure the deliverer will have information on risk: participants will be able to say if the training feels too threatening. You will also be building in the feedback channel which allows the deliverer generally to manoeuvre to meet the participants' needs.

Balance theory and practice

Participants generally expect some kind of theoretical underpinning to training. You will lose credibility if it is totally skills and practice. Too much theory switches people off, though.

In a two-day interviewing programme, I would typically include four 20-minute inputs on the principles of good interviewing, plus half an hour on interesting research findings. The best theory of all is theory which shocks and/or entertains. For example, the following research finding is a great stimulus to learning:

> most selection decisions are made by the untrained interviewer in the first five seconds of the interview

The balance of theory and practice needs to take into account the background and interests of the participants. But be warned: people sometimes ask for a lot of theory, but in practice end up bored and disappointed by it. They are often hoping for absolute proof of the leadership style which works best, or a cast-iron recipe for building a successful team. Since no such things exist, it is better to give them a short burst of the theory which does exist, and lots of practice.

Design in feedback

> Call to mind feedback you have had during your career that has made a difference to you. You may be surprised at the vividness with which you recall examples of praise or criticism.

When it comes to behaviour change and skills development, feedback is an absolute prerequisite for learning. Not only that, it is the single training element which most increases individual commitment. When I start to get feedback on how I am doing, then I really believe the training is for me.

Seeking, giving and getting feedback are also risky activities for people. You can sense the increased level of apprehension when feedback sessions are about to start. It is therefore an invaluable tool for increasing risk. (I usually judge whether a teambuilding programme has been a success or not by whether I feel it is 'safe' to ask team members to give each other feedback on their impact in the team.) So the training designer should be looking to complete the feedback loop as often as possible.

One note of caution: it is not generally a good idea to design for the trainer giving the feedback. It is too powerful an experience for most participants, and also it disturbs the helpful, facilitatory role that trainers try to establish. It makes them look like judges, and it can take people inappropriately back to the days of school and teacher. So design sessions where participants give each other feedback. Give them precise questions to answer for each other, as in Table 17.

Table 17

DESIGN FOR FEEDBACK SESSION ON PRESENTATION SKILLS

Do not say	Do say
'Give presenters feedback on their presentation.'	'Give presenters feedback on their presentation by answering these questions:
	▪ What did they do that made you feel they were talking to you?
	▪ What did they do that kept your attention?
	▪ Was there anything they could have done differently to get your attention more?'

(The trainer will almost inevitably be asked for feedback. I cannot count, for example, the number of teams who have asked me on teambuilding programmes: 'Are we the worst team you've ever worked with?' 'What do you think of us as a team, really?' But what the group really needs from the trainer when they ask questions like this are not detailed points but general reassurance. And this applies to individuals who corner the trainer too. The skilled deliverer will know how to give feedback which reassures honestly, without straying into specific coaching, and will also know how to turn the group and individuals in the group back towards each other for the points of detail.)

Design for closure

Participants need to feel that a training programme has a beginning, a middle and an end. At the end, they need to feel a sense of closure, a satisfaction that something useful has now been completed.

The commonest method of achieving this is the action planning session. Participants summarise what they will do differently as a result of the training, and present their action plans to each other. Certainly the training designer should include at some point near the end a session where what has been learned is made explicit and specific.

But there are some more interesting ways to design a close which increases commitment and attention to the learning right to the end of the programme and beyond. Here are some:

- an entertainment, designed and put on by participants for tutors, with some relevance to the course content
- presentation of certificates or awards (serious or fun!)
- closing speeches (serious or fun!)
- closing feedback by group members to each other: 'What I have learned from you in these two days is that …'
- presentation of gifts (for example, a book of the course, an apple for the trainer!).

In brief

- The training designer must ask five key questions at all times about every element of the training:
  - ☐ is it credible
  - ☐ will it win the commitment of participants
  - ☐ does it manage the risk to which participants are exposed in a way which is helpful to their learning
  - ☐ will it win and keep their attention
  - ☐ will it give the trainer room to manoeuvre in response to what is going on in and outside the training room?

- In order to answer 'yes' to all these questions, the training designer should use 10 fundamental principles in the design:
  - ☐ Maximise action and interaction. This is the classic way to keep people's attention and build their commitment.
  - ☐ Signpost, signpost and then signpost again. Participants need to be absolutely clear at all times about why they are doing what they're doing.
  - ☐ Vary pace and rhythm. The more interesting the music, the more attention people will pay to it.
  - ☐ Chunk content. Attention rises at beginnings and ends. Build lots of beginnings and ends into your training.
  - ☐ Map the participants' world. Meet them where they are, talk their language and they will listen.
  - ☐ Give participants choices. If you treat them as colleagues, they will react as colleagues.
  - ☐ Surface objections. When participants have objections to the training, those objections need to be heard by the trainer so that they can be addressed and the group can move on, without leaving people behind.

☐ Balance theory and practice. Some theory is nearly always a good idea. Too much is always disastrous.

☐ Design in feedback. People learn more through feedback than through anything else. And it grips their attention.

☐ Design for closure. Make sure participants will leave the training with a sense of completion, of achievement.

6 Playing with Process

Introduction

It has been a recurrent theme of this book that in training 'it ain't what you do, it's the way that you do it'. In other words, how you position the training in the organisation, who you invite, and background choices on such things as venue and use of IT are at least as important in determining training outcome as the content of the programme. In this chapter, we explore this theme even further. We discuss how the nature of interactions between participants influences hugely what people learn, and how, by treating that process of interaction as another significant leverage point in training design, the designer suddenly discovers a whole new dimension of intervention to play with. You can think of the training designer, learning the craft, as passing through three developmental stages. In the first, the focus is on the relationship between participants and training content. Is it clear enough? Is it interesting enough? Has the right amount of information and the right pace of activity been provided? In the second developmental stage, the focus widens to include the relationship between participants and training deliverer. Has the design permitted the establishment of trust? Does the deliverer have the flexibility to respond to different groups' needs? In the third and final stage, the designer widens the focus yet again to include the relationships between participants. It is with this third and final stage that the present chapter is concerned.

The small-group approach

In the small-group approach, the training is designed so that there are two equally important mechanisms for learning running in parallel. One is the programme itself, with its sequence of inputs from the tutor, discussions and exercises. The second is the evolution of teamworking in a number of small stable sub-groups into which the participants are divided and in which they work for certain tasks throughout the programme.

This type of design is particularly effective when the subject of the training is closely related to effectiveness in group work. Examples would be interpersonal skills training, teamworking training and leadership training. Table 18 on page 84 shows, for each of these examples, how the small group approach offers particularly relevant learning opportunities.

An innovative use of the small-group approach

I have seen the small group approach used very effectively in the design of a customer service programme for a major high street retailer. It was in some ways a surprising choice of approach since the relevance of group dynamics to customer service is not immediately apparent. But the logic behind the design choice was in fact sound.

First, good customer service in the stores depended ultimately on a team approach from everyone working in a particular store. Secondly, good customer service depended on each employee being aware of his impact on people and knowing how to improve that impact. Where better to get feedback on that than in the context of the small group? Thirdly, in the small group, the other members of your group are in one sense your customers. Sometimes they will be demanding, infuriating, unreasonable. Throughout you have to work with them to get an outcome which suits everyone. The skills you need to use to achieve this are exactly the skills you need with external customers.

Table 18

SMALL-GROUP LEARNING OPPORTUNITIES

Type of training	What can be learned in small groups
Interpersonal skills	In the small group, each individual must build effective working relationships quickly. Usually, the small group will consist of relative 'strangers' who can give each other feedback on how they interact and coach each other in interacting more effectively.
Teamworking	The small group must become a team to carry out the required tasks in the programme. As the programme progresses, the 'teams' will go through the usual stages of team development, in accelerated fashion. So the members will learn about these stages, and how to respond to them. They will experience the group dynamics of teamworking at first hand, and be able to reflect on how the theory of the programme content is demonstrated in practice in their own teams.
Leadership	Each participant takes it in turns to lead their small group for a task. Their experiences are used to illustrate and bring to life the programme content. Also, they can try out different leadership approaches and get feedback. The opportunity both to lead and to be part of the group when it is being led by someone else is quite rare and usually gives rise to some very sharp insights into the whole business of leadership.

So the three-day programme contained tutor inputs on assertiveness, customer survey results, impression management (with particular reference to store layout), 'moments of truth' (that is, key interactions between retailer and customer which determine buying behaviour), and other customer service topics, interspersed with small-group work on tasks related to the inputs and review sessions on the group work. Over four hundred people participated in the programme; and they reported that the element they learned most from was the small-group working.

A variation on the small-group theme

When I was asked to design a teamworking programme for part of a large industrial company, it rapidly became clear that people had no difficulty in forming small close-knit teams. The problem was in fact quite the reverse: people had a very bad record of co-operating with people from other teams. This was a serious problem, since the design and production process depended heavily on good between-team co-operation.

I puzzled over how to design a training programme which brought about better between-team co-operation. Clearly the classic small-group approach wouldn't do: it would just exacerbate the problem.

Eventually I decided upon a variation on the small-group approach which would require people to confront – and solve – the problem of building so much loyalty to a single team that it inhibits effective working outside the team. I designed a series of small group tasks (interspersed as usual with relevant inputs) in which groups competed with each other. Half-way through the programme, the composition of the small groups was changed. Success depended then on co-operating quickly with people that you had previously been competing with.

This small-group experience provided many opportunities for participants to gain insights into what was impeding between-team co-operation in the workplace. It was practically and impressively demonstrated that some of the 'best' team players in the first part of the programme were 'worst' at forming new teams in the second part. This led to discussion on how they could get the best of both worlds – good team work and good between-teams work – and to specific action planning to improve things in the workplace.

Dos and don'ts of the small-group approach

Here are some tips to help you make best use of the small-group approach.

- *Don't* confuse it with straightforward syndicate working or break-out groups (see Chapter 5, page 68). The whole essence of the small group approach is that the groups stay the same throughout the programme (unless they are changed specifically in order to break the continuity, as in the teamworking example described above). With syndicates and break-out groups, the idea is to shuffle the pack of participants constantly, creating variety and interaction which promote the 'primary' learning (that is, learning via the programme itself). With the small-group approach, the idea is to establish a second parallel track of learning, additional to the primary learning.

- *Do* provide in the design for each small group to have a skilled facilitator or tutor, to help them in group reviews and feedback sessions. Not only will many learning opportunities be lost if you don't do this, but interactions within the group can become destructive and inappropriately emotional if no one is there to watch over the process. You should include in your design a clear statement of the purpose of each small group session, and of how the group tutor should facilitate achievement of that purpose.

> Have you ever been the victim of 'bad group dynamics'? You may, for example, have worked in a team that had two members who were constantly at each other's throats. You will have experienced embarrassment or frustration. You may have felt the 'odd one out' in a team. That feeling will have sapped your ability to contribute. Thinking about the power of bad group dynamics will alert you to the need to avoid this in your training design.

- *Don't* allow the groups to be so focused on task (that is, on competing with each other) that they neglect to learn from *how* they are working together. Design into the timetable specific group sessions where there is no task other than to discuss the group's process (that is, its way of working – its functioning as a team).

- *Do* pay attention to the size of the small groups. Six to eight is ideal; fewer, and the group may lack energy and interactive opportunity; more, and the group risks becoming a committee.

- *Don't* design so much time in small groups that the integrity and cohesiveness of the programme is lost. Participants need to feel they were all basically on the same course! Also, some groups will inevitably be more rewarding to be in than others. You need to ensure in your design that no one is likely to be trapped in a 'bad' group (boring, hostile, unsympathetic) for too high a proportion of the course time. (This is not a problem with syndicates and break-out groups because participants are constantly changing groups.)

The facilitation approach

The term 'facilitation' literally means 'making things easier'. Facilitation in the sense of helping others to do something in a new way is used all over organisations, inside and outside the training suite, and in as many different ways as there are new approaches to be introduced. Some organisations will train a group of in-house facilitators at times of great change, for example – and these facilitators will roam around the organisation, looking for any ways they can help, support and coach individuals and teams to meet the changing requirements.

I shall be using the term 'facilitation' in a narrower sense here. I want to explore how the training designer can build into his programmes sessions where the training deliverer coaches the whole group or parts of the group in using a new approach, by interacting with them as they try it out. Let me give you an example.

Using a facilitation session to teach 'brainstorming'

Suppose one of the training programme objectives is to impart the principles and skills of 'brainstorming'. One design approach would be to explain briefly the origins and uses of brainstorming, by means of a group discussion, to summarise and give to participants the 'brainstorming rules', and then send them off in small groups to try a brainstorm and give each other feedback on how well they kept to the rules. The session would conclude with a discussion of what they had learned, and where they thought they could use brainstorming at work. Later sessions in the programme could be used to give them more practice.

This piece of training might be significantly enhanced by a session in which the deliverer 'facilitates' the whole group as it conducts a brainstorm. She ensures the rules are kept to and intervenes when they are not. ('No evaluation'; 'Make sure every idea goes up on the flipchart'.) She may take on the role of flipchart scribe to help out and to model the right way to do it. She may intervene to raise the energy level of the group. ('Keep the ideas coming!'; 'Let's have some crazy ideas!'; 'What's the craziest thing you can think of?')

This type of facilitation enhances skills development in four ways. Firstly, participants are helped to get the new skill right as they're actually trying it out. Hopefully good habits will be established early on. Secondly, it can be less threatening for participants to be coached by the tutor before trying a new skill out on their own. Thirdly, example is usually a much better means of communicating a new skill than description. Lastly, the tutor acts as a powerful model of the new technique.

Facilitation sessions of this type can be used effectively for most skills development. If the skill is not one that can be practised in a group (for example, personal objective

Chartered Institute of Personnel and Development

Customer Satisfaction Survey

We would be grateful if you could spend a few minutes answering these questions and return the postcard to CIPD. <u>Please use a black pen to answer</u>. **If you would like to receive a free CIPD pen, please include your name and address.** IPD MEMBER Y/N

....

1. Title of book ....

2. Date of purchase: month .... year ....

3. How did you acquire this book?
☐Bookshop ☐Mail order ☐Exhibition ☐Gift ☐Bought from Author

4. If ordered by mail, how long did it take to arrive:
☐1 week ☐2 weeks ☐more than 2 weeks

5. Name of shop .... Town.. Country............

6. Please grade the following according to their influence on your purchasing decision with 1 as least influential: (please tick)

	1	2	3	4	5
Title					
Publisher					
Author					
Price					
Subject					
Cover					

7. On a scale of 1 to 5 (with 1 as poor & 5 as excellent) please give your impressions of the book in terms of: (please tick)

	1	2	3	4	5
Cover design					
Paper/print quality					
Good value for money					
General level of service					

8. Did you find the book:

Covers the subject in sufficient depth ☐Yes ☐No
Useful for your work ☐Yes ☐No

9. Are you using this book to help:
☐In your work ☐Personal study ☐Both ☐Other (please state)

Please complete if you are using this as part of a course

10. Name of academic institution...

11. Name of course you are following? ....

12. Did you find this book relevant to the syllabus? ☐Yes ☐No ☐Don't know

Thank you!

To receive regular information about CIPD books and resources call 020 8263 3387.

Any data or information provided to the CIPD for the purposes of membership and other Institute activities will be processed by means of a computer database or otherwise. You may, from time to time, receive business information relevant to your work from the Institute and its other activities. If you do not wish to receive such information please write to the CIPD, giving your full name, address and postcode. The Institute does not make its membership lists available to any outside organisation.

1795/05/00

Publishing Department

Chartered Institute of Personnel and Development

CIPD House

Camp Road

Wimbledon

London

SW19 4BR

setting), then you can design in a session where the tutor facilitates one participant in front of the group. (Of course, the tutor will have to ask for volunteers, and not impose that degree of exposure on anyone.)

You might be wondering whether you should ever *not* use facilitation sessions. Do not use them when participants do not need them – when they are perfectly capable of trying a skill out as soon as it has been explained. Facilitation would seem patronising. Also, beware of using it too much. It can increase the extent to which the participants rely on the tutor, and decrease the extent to which they learn from each other. Lastly, do not ask deliverers to do anything which is beyond their competence. Facilitation is more demanding than most other training elements, because it requires deliverers to be skilled in whichever approach they are communicating and to be able to think and respond on their feet to what is happening in the group.

The 'direct process manipulation' approach

With 'direct process manipulation', you set specific rules for process which will result in participants learning new behaviour. The rules are often unusual, requiring participants to operate outside their normal behavioural range and so establish new habits and/or gain insights into the consequences of their usual behaviour. Two examples should make this approach clearer.

The over-argumentative managers

I had been asked to design a culture change programme for a large group of senior managers. They would attend the programme in groups of twenty.

One of their key issues was an inability to achieve consensus and then 'cabinet responsibility' across the management group. Whenever one of them presented an idea or a proposal, others would destroy it critically. I debated whether to include sessions on consultation, decision-making, and management responsibility; and decided against it. These were sophisticated people, perfectly capable of pulling any amount of theory to pieces and continuing to argue and debate to the detriment of quality management dialogue.

I decided to design a series of sessions where artificial rules were imposed on the discussion process such that managers would experience a different way of exploring issues and coming to conclusions. In one session, for example, the rule was that a specified half of the group was allowed to make suggestions and provide information (this half all had experience of the issue under discussion); the other half were only allowed to ask questions seeking clarification or further information. They were not allowed to put forward counter-proposals, or to dispute the information given.

In this session, participants discovered they learned more about the experience of the information-giving half than they would had they dived into their customary debate. The information-giving half felt their points had been truly understood. The two halves were subsequently able to reach agreement on a related policy issue.

In another session, the imposed rule was: 'You may not speak for longer than 30 seconds at a time'. Participants were amazed at how rapidly they could make their points, in this discipline!

The team that did not listen

I recently did some team training with a small group of very extrovert and vocal directors. They had asked for a session on listening skills – recognising they rarely listened to each other. I responded by designing a session where they discussed a key company issue on which they had to make some decisions, but they discussed it using an artificial process. For the first 45 minutes, half the team discussed; the other half sat round them and took notes.

For the next 45 minutes, roles were reversed, but the discussion had to be a continuation from the point the first group had reached, not a going-over of old ground. So the process went on, throughout the morning, sub-groups taking it in turns to discuss and listen.

The most striking thing for these directors was the enormous contrast between this process and their normal process: interrupting, talking over each other, private conversations on the side. It gave them a real experiential insight into how things could be different.

Dos and don'ts of the direct process manipulation approach

Here are some tips to help you make best use of this approach.

■ *Do* include in your design an explanation to the participants of where and why direct process manipulation is to be used. Participants should be willing collaborators, and not feel that they are being manipulated.

■ *Don't* ask an inexperienced training deliverer to operate unusual process rules. It often takes a very experienced and confident trainer to inspire confidence in the group to experiment and do 'strange things'.

> Imagine you could have a skilled facilitator at one meeting you regularly attend. Which meeting would you choose? Why? What would you hope the facilitator would achieve? What challenges would the facilitator have to face?

■ *Do* vary process rules throughout a training day to increase variety and hold attention (remember Chapter 5 has more detail on 'attention' as an important training parameter).

■ *Don't* allow the manipulation of process to be seen as 'unfair', that is, favouring the interests of some participants over others. So, for example, if in one session only half the group is allowed to brainstorm, there must be a later session where the other half brainstorms.

The two-tutor approach

You may remember that in Chapter 2 I discussed briefly the benefits and costs of having a two-tutor team (see page 26). I referred briefly to the 'possibility of humour and interest in a double act'.

When it comes to playing with process, this possibility becomes very attractive indeed. Let's look at two aspects of its attractiveness.

Facilitating facilitation

I have already commented on the fact that the delivery skills required for some of the training approaches outlined in this chapter are advanced. Direct process manipulation is particularly demanding. There is a high risk that the group will 'turn against' the deliverer and blame him or her for any failures in their learning or shortcomings in their performance. The group is always close to the edge, willing to co-operate so long as the deliverer is communicating confidence and support, ready to dive into 'you set these ridiculous rules, you can take the consequences' at the slightest crack in the deliverer's competence.

But with a two-tutor team, this collapse of group confidence in the deliverer is much less likely to happen. Not only do the two tutors support each other and thus make the group feel safer, but they can take it in turns to make inputs to the group, allowing each other much more thinking time than either would have alone.

A two-tutor team can simply share the facilitation role, as equal partners. But they can provide for even more flexibility of approach and impact on the group by working together asymmetrically. One very powerful approach which I have seen work extremely well in direct process manipulation is where one tutor interacts directly with the group and the partner adopts a supervisory role, observing the session for most of the time, perhaps taking notes. Every so often, when the group is getting on with a task, they discuss what is going on and jointly plan the next session. This approach is extremely effective in helping the up-front partner maintain objectivity and detachment, even when dealing with the most fraught group dynamics.

At the other end of the sophistication spectrum it is amazing how supportive and confidence-building it is to have a colleague simply sitting at the side of the room, nodding every so often when you make a particularly good point. I have a colleague who is very generous with his nods, and I have noticed over the years how the minute he walks into a room, the delivery of the tutor standing at the front goes up a notch in terms of self-assurance and impact.

Modelling process

The second attractive aspect of the two-tutor team is the opportunity it gives the tutors to model, in the dynamic between them, key process points which the group itself is trying to learn.

Let me give you a concrete example. Imagine a two-tutor team conducting a piece of teambuilding with a group that were constantly finding fault with each other's points. A key process skill that the team needs to learn is that of 'building', of making a new point in a way which identifies what is right with a previous point rather than in a way which identifies what is wrong with it. Table 19 illustrates 'building', and its opposite. (In the West, partly because of certain conventions in our education system and philosophical tradition, we are generally much more skilled at 'knocking down' than at 'building'.)

Table 19

'KNOCKING-DOWN' AND 'BUILDING' DIALOGUE

Knocking-down	Building
A: 'We should form a task force to address this issue.'	A: 'We should form a task force to address this issue.'
B: 'The last task force was a complete waste of time.'	B: 'I like the idea of a focused group. I wonder if we could call it something different.'
A: 'No one's suggesting we should do it the same way as last time. For a start, it needs to meet regularly.'	A: 'Perhaps you're right. After all, the last "task force" wasn't exactly a success.'
B: 'It never will. The whole problem is that no one has the time for task-force activities.'	B: 'Yes, I've got a feeling it was simply never given enough resource.'
A: 'That's such a defeatist attitude – and it's typical of you.'	A: 'Maybe if we called it a project team but defined the project in very specific terms we could get resource via the project control system.'
B: 'I sometimes wonder when you're going to join the real world.'	B: 'Good idea. Our main problem then is going to be convincing senior management that people need time for this.'
	A: 'I'll raise it with the MD at our meeting tomorrow.'

The two-tutor team can model 'building' dialogue not only during the session focused specifically on that but throughout the programme. They can build on each other's comments and avoid destructive challenge. It is often the implicit example of a different process being lived out in front of them which encourages people to experiment with doing things differently. This is a much more powerful inducement to learning than any explicit exhortation to change. The group may or may not comment on the fact that the tutors are practising what they preach; but the dynamic of the two-tutor team will in either case provide for truly multidimensional learning.

Professional partners, not chums

There are two great risks in two-tutor teams, and one is much more insidious than the other. The first risk, more easily perceived and dealt with, is that the tutors will fall out. One executive I worked with on a culture change programme had been on a four-week-long 'top manager' course after his promotion from middle to senior management. He rated the course highly and was still using things he had learned on it five years later. But the story he told most frequently and most readily about it had nothing to do with its content: it had everything to do with the fact that the two tutors who delivered it, in his words, 'hated each other's guts'. Their barely concealed sparring, and competing with each other had been a source of much amusement to the participants, and must have detracted from their learning.

If you fall out with a fellow deliverer, either resolve your problem quickly or agree at least not to work with each other until you have. Training delivery is difficult enough without an 'enemy within'.

Now let us turn to the second, more insidious, risk. This is that the tutors become too chummy, that they collude in order to make life easier for each other rather than co-operate in order to make learning more effective for the participants. What are the signs of collusion?

- The tutors never challenge each other, never constructively criticise each other's delivery, even in private.
- The tutors criticise the participants when they are alone and, when the training goes wrong, they unite in blaming the group.
- The tutors feel the same emotions at the same time: when one is optimistic, so is the other; when one is down, both are.
- The tutors get too close: they socialise more with each other than with the participants; they have a lot of in-jokes; they look like 'buddies', not like a professional team.

■ The participants think they must be having an affair.

Of course, to work as an effective two-tutor team, the deliverers must understand each other's style, build a working relationship, and agree on many aspects of their approach to training. But their co-tutoring relationship must be maintained in order to provide a better service to the group and not for their own gratification.

In brief

■ The training designer can include to great effect sessions in the programme which encourage or inhibit certain types of interaction between participants. These are often called 'process interventions'.

■ Three of the most frequently used are:
  ◻ small-group work
  ◻ facilitation
  ◻ direct process manipulation.

■ In small-group work, participants learn from being part of a developing team which carries out many tasks and activities during the programme. Small-group work is particularly useful when the subject of the training relates closely to interpersonal skills or teamworking.

■ In facilitation, the trainer coaches the group of participants directly in new skills and approaches, interacting with them as they try these skills and approaches out, helping them to master them more quickly and more completely. Facilitation is particularly useful when people are learning something which cannot be easily prescribed.

■ In direct process manipulation, the training imposes rules which change the nature of interactions between participants. It is particularly useful to break old habits.

■ A two-tutor team offers scope for increased interest and impact through the tutors modelling new processes in their own dynamic, and supporting each other to engage in more challenging work with the group.

■ All the process interventions described in this chapter require skilled and experienced training deliverers, facilitation and direct process manipulation particularly.

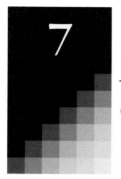

7

Mixed Personality Classes

Introduction

Training is usually conducted with a group of people, for reasons of efficiency, and also because the group itself provides extra opportunities for learning (see Chapter 6). But the group approach brings with it problems as well as opportunities (in Chapter 5, for example, I discussed the issue of participants being embarrassed to experiment in front of an audience.) The problem we are going to explore in this chapter is the problem of a group being composed of individuals, each of whom learns in their own way, at their own pace, and who cannot be treated for training purposes as an undifferentiated entity. A training element which may be ideal for the risk-taking socialite may be disastrously inappropriate for the cautious loner. (Such an element would be: making an after dinner speech on things you have learned during the programme!)

The diversity of the group is at best consciously exploited by the training designer for extra training impact. But at the very least it must be taken into account. Otherwise you will be relying on the personality and ingenuity of the training deliverer alone to make the training work for very different people. You may end up with your deliverer having to 'fight with' the design to ensure participants are not alienated or left behind, when your design should have been supporting his or her efforts to make the training work for everyone.

Some general points

Shortly we shall look at specific dimensions of difference between people of which the training designer should be aware. But first let us consider some general principles of training design that make a training intervention more likely to work for a 'mixed group', that is, for a variety of styles, abilities and preferences. We discuss the two most important of these now.

Give participants choices

You may remember this as one of the 10 fundamental design principles in Chapter 5. The more choices you design into the programme, the more likely there will be enough in it that suits everyone. This will particularly be true if the choices you give people account for the major differences in learning style that are likely to exist in a group. We talk more about these differences below, but for now let me give you one specific example of a programme which was well designed in this respect.

The programme was a career development workshop for senior managers in an international archiving organisation. Whilst there were some individuals in the population who were very sociable and open, many were the classic 'literary, scholarly types': shy, private, highly reflective and analytical, preferring to work for much of their time in a solitary way. After all, their backgrounds were in librarianship, archiving, and historical research. For logistical reasons the programme had to be delivered to twenty senior managers at a time. Also, some people in the organisation wanted the programme to promote more co-operation and communication between senior managers if possible. But the primary objective was for each senior manager to come away with his own personal development plan, to which he was committed. The training methods were not to get in the way of that.

So the training was designed to allow a great deal of individual choice about whether to work in private study, in pairs, in small groups, or in the whole group. Inputs on the different elements of personal development planning were delivered to the whole group. In those sessions, participants could choose whether to listen quietly or participate in discussion and exploration of their own case. Each input was followed by a session in which any one participant could choose whether to join a group (run by one of the tutors) or whether to work alone or in pairs and 'book' a short piece of time with the other tutor.

The design of this programme meant everyone could choose the way of working which suited them best. No one was preoccupied with being forced to be more open than felt comfortable or helpful. People could concentrate on achieving the programme objective in their own way, supported by the tutors in whichever way they chose.

Design training in layers

There will be parts of any training programme to which everyone is exposed, such as the tutor's presentations to the whole group. But there are other parts which some of the participants may not even be aware of, unless they need to be. So you can visualise a piece of training design as a stack of layers: participants choose how deep they go.

Let me give you a specific example. When I design teambuilding training, I know that some people will only be interested in sorting out their own team very immediately and very practically. This is usually the primary objective of the intervention, and is the top layer. Everyone will participate in sessions, discussing team strengths and weaknesses, giving each other feedback, and planning for improvement.

But some theoretically inclined people will want to think more broadly about teamworking. They will want to know about concepts such as the 'high performing team' and the 'self-managed team'. They will want to read a bit of the research. So I will put together a reading list about these things, and suggest in the tutor notes that a book-table be provided during the workshop with some or all of the books on the list available for people to dip into. This is a second layer of training, into which only some participants will dive.

I am also aware that some participants will particularly want to compare and contrast their own team with practical and recent examples from other organisations. So I will include some case studies in the course notes, to which the deliverer can draw people's attention, if they are interested. Some participants will read these, and maybe discuss them with the tutor over dinner. This is another layer of the training. (The use of course materials to enrich the layered nature of training in this way is described more fully in another book in this series: *Developing Learning Materials* by Jacqui Gough.)

Finally, I know that some participants – again, not all – will want to consider the implications of what they have learned in the team sessions for their personal development. So I will design a couple of 'surgery' sessions, where participants can book individual time with the tutor. Meanwhile, the other participants will be relaxing or reading. Here is yet another layer to the training.

The layered approach to training design gives the training a multidimensionality which mirrors and matches the multidimensionality of the group.

The most important differences

We shall now look at some specific dimensions of difference which impact heavily on the type of training which works best for different individuals. If you as a training designer bear at least these in mind in the choices you give participants and the layers you design, you will go a long way towards meeting the needs of the 'mixed personality class'.

There are a number of models of 'learning styles' (the most important differences between people which determine how they learn). The best known of these is Honey and Mumford's Learning Styles, a model which has been used successfully and enthusiastically in organisations for many years. I personally prefer to think about my 'mixed personality classes' within the framework of the Myers-Briggs Type Inventory, a model of individual differences in thinking and problem-solving style which has strong links with Honey and Mumford's Learning Styles but which is relevant to more aspects of an individual's mental functioning than learning alone. It is simple but fundamental, and based on Jung's original work on cognitive types.

In fact, I think it is more important for a training designer to have some framework for understanding individual differences in learning than to use any particular one. For any framework will alert you to the key fact that a training intervention must engage in a variety of ways, at a range of levels, if it is to engage a group of individuals. You will probably evolve your own framework, if you haven't already, based on the sorts of groups you design for (see also Chapter 1, the section on 'Imagining the participants', pages 15–16). But the framework I offer you here is based on the Myers-Briggs. It is summarised in Figure 4.

Figure 4

HOW PEOPLE LEARN: A FRAMEWORK OF THE MOST IMPORTANT DIFFERENCES

Each individual will occupy a specific position on each of the four dimensions. (I am, for example, an extrovert, concept-loving, logic-led, fluid learner.)

extrovert	*as opposed to*	introvert
evidence-seeking	*as opposed to*	concept-loving
logic-led	*as opposed to*	values-driven
structured	*as opposed to*	fluid

As you read the following pages, ask yourself which end of each dimension best describes you. Knowing your own learning preferences will help you both *use* these preferences and avoid *over*using them in the training you design. If you have very extreme preferences, you might like to get your training designs checked out by colleagues with different preferences, to ensure they cover all the styles participants might prefer.

Extrovert v introvert learners

Each of these dimensions is a spectrum, but to clarify the picture I shall describe the two extremes. Most people are clearly one side or the other. Extrovert learners have all or some of the following characteristics:

∎ They like to experiment and try out new skills and approaches. They will not feel they have learned something until they have experienced how it works. They like to learn through action.

∎ They like to learn with others, developing their own thinking through talking with others, learning how they are getting on by experiencing others' reactions. They thrive on feedback. They like to learn through interaction.

∎ They prefer learning things which make a visible, or tangible difference.

∎ They will get bored or tired by spending too much time learning on their own.

Introvert learners have, in contrast, all or some of these characteristics:

∎ They like to reflect on new skills and approaches. They may need encouragement to try them out, and will want to feel they have gained a degree of mastery through reflection before experimenting actively.

∎ They do much of their learning privately, even when

in the midst of others. They may surprise others by the individualistic insights they come out with, after a prolonged period of quiet. It is easy to mistake their lack of audible or visible participation for lack of interest. In fact, their silence often means intense interest.

■ They are happy to acquire new information or ideas which 'may come in useful later'. They enjoy simply enriching their inner life.

■ They will get cumulatively stressed by a high quantity of action and interaction. They will need recovery time.

You will already have spotted that some of the ways introvert and extrovert learners should be catered for in training design have been described in the 'career development workshop' example earlier in this chapter (page 99). Most training is much more suited to the extrovert learner. Not only is the group setting more to the extrovert learner's taste, but 60 per cent of the population are extrovert learners, and an even higher proportion of managers, so most groups tend to have a definitely extrovert atmosphere. As a designer of training you should make positive efforts to include elements of reflection for the introvert learner. (Extroverts benefit too, if you can get them to sit still!)

Evidence-seeking v concept-loving learners

The evidence-seekers are the 'doubting Thomases' of the training room. They like proof, examples, demonstration that what they are learning is tried and tested. Evidence-seeking learners have all or some of the following characteristics:

■ They like to see the step-by-step logic behind what they are learning.

■ They prefer to try something out *after* they have assured themselves that it works, and that it is useful.

■ They like to know about the evidence behind a new approach: they will typically ask questions such as

'Where has this been shown to work? Can you give me examples of people who have used this successfully?'

∎ They are impressed by real-life examples, unimpressed by theory and 'new-fangled ideas'.

Concept-loving learners are often impatient with all these things so beloved of the evidence-seeker. They have some or all of the following characteristics:

∎ They enjoy new ideas for their own sake, whether or not they can see an immediate practical application.

∎ They like concepts, patterns, links – and so they actually like theory. They will even put up with jargon, if the ideas behind the jargon capture their imagination.

∎ They are more interested in future possibilities than past events. They are prepared to give a new approach a go, to experiment, to take things on trust.

∎ They can welcome change simply because it is change. At worst, they tend to be dilettante; at best they are true innovators and enthusiasts for development.

The key to designing training which works for both evidence-seekers and concept-lovers is as follows. When you want to introduce a new approach, idea or skill, begin with a small amount of evidence and fact. For example, a good opener for an interviewing skills course is a statistic such as 'Research suggests that interviewing skills training doubles the validity of the interviewer's recruitment decisions'. The facts will engage the evidence-seeker but not be in so much detail that they bore the concept-lover. Provide a fact-sheet with further relevant statistics (see pages 100–101 on designing training in layers), and then move on to some key concepts. Then you can go into the practical session confident that both the evidence-seekers and the concept-lovers will be with you.

Logic-led v values-driven learners

Some people learn more with their heads ('logic-led'), others more with their hearts ('values-driven'). Logic-led learners are often:

▪ detached
▪ concerned about task accomplishment
▪ tough-minded
▪ focused on analytical rigour
▪ challenging of the thinking behind training.

Values-driven learners are often:

▪ emotionally bound-up with their learning
▪ concerned about people's feelings
▪ disturbed by conflict
▪ focused on people's reactions (their own, their fellow participants', their colleagues' back at work)
▪ challenging of the values behind training.

What the existence of these two perspectives on learning means for the training designer is that both the intellectual credibility of the training and also its ethical credibility must be established.

I once designed a training intervention on project management skills in which I forgot the values side of the equation. I am myself 'logic-led', so it is harder for me to remember it; also, because the subject of the training seemed so task-focused, I was even less aware of the values issues than usual. I used two artificial tasks for people to try out their project management skills on – they were meant to be fun, very participative, and yet provide some useful learning opportunities on the subject of organising others. One task was building a bridge out of newspaper which would be strong enough to support a tutor's weight. Another task was building a tower, as high as possible with very few materials.

The organisation for whom I designed the course was very keen to promote equal opportunities. It had had a somewhat troubled history of subtle prejudice against promoting women into senior positions, and was just beginning to overcome the legacy of that prejudice. In the group of managers who attended the project management skills course were two or three values-driven learners who were particularly concerned with the value of fairness and equal opportunity for women.

They reacted strongly against the artificial tasks. They considered they were both very 'masculine' in nature, focusing as they did on engineering, construction, and 'doing things with your hands.'

I took their point. But the reason I relate this story here is to emphasise that there are no short-cuts to appealing to the values-driven learner. You need to be sensitive to the key values of the people who will be attending your programme, and at the very least avoid offending those values. At best, you will use case studies, examples and practical exercises which appeal to their values set, and so enhance the effectiveness of your training. (The section on designing training with integrity in Chapter 3, – pages 44 46 – is also relevant here.)

Structured v fluid learners

This dimension is relevant principally not to the content of the training, but to its organisation. Structured learners like to know where they are going, get there, and then know where they have been. When it comes to signposting (see Chapter 5, the ten fundamental design principles), they need even more of it than the average participant. They like training with the following characteristics:

- regular, predictable structure
- very clearly stated objectives, clear links between content and objectives, and review sessions against objectives
- specific action-planning sessions
- summaries of learning points, practical check-lists, guidance notes
- a definite end.

Fluid learners are less demanding in many ways. They are 'learning magpies', picking things up opportunistically, enjoying a certain amount of chaos and spontaneity. They rather enjoy changes to the programme, and they are prepared to embark on an activity without always knowing what it is intended to achieve. They may become suspicious or bored if everything runs too smoothly; they may feel cramped by the kinds of things structured learners appreciate.

Of all the dimensions, this one is the most difficult to design successfully for both ends of. The best combination is a structured modular design with an experienced, flexible deliverer. That way, the deliverer can respond to the particular combination of learning preferences in each group he delivers the training to. For a very structured group, he can stick to the timetable strictly; for a very fluid group, he can insert more open exploratory sessions, follow the participants' interests, and adjust timings accordingly.

The thing to remember is that the structured learner is on a course in order to achieve an output. They will be looking all the time for proof that the output is coming. The fluid learner is on a course at least in part to enjoy the process, the journey. They will be prepared to take the output on trust, providing the process is interesting. If you follow the ten fundamental design principles in Chapter 5, you will not disappoint either of them too much.

Mixed 'ability' classes

One of the most refreshing facts about training is that 'ability' in the academic sense seems to matter much less than it does in formal education. Most of the subject matter which training addresses is very practical (see Chapter 1 on 'Understanding Training'). It does not have to be learned through the intellectual mastery of complex concepts, nor through memorising vast quantities of data. In fact, too much intellectualisation is inimical to the kind of practical learning in which training deals.

Can you identify training courses you have been on where you had the opportunity to learn from people with very different educational backgrounds from yourself? What was it in the design of those courses which facilitated that kind of learning?

So in my experience mixed ability classes are not a problem. In fact, they present a variety of opportunities to the training designer:

■ an opportunity to include discussion sessions between participants in which the 'more intellectual' intrigue others with their knowledge of, and interest in, the theoretical base and objective justification of new approaches, while the 'less intellectual' maintain the focus on practical application; when 'book-learning' meets 'streetwise' the results can be considerably more than the sum of the parts

■ an opportunity to design in layers (see pages 100–101) to reflect different degrees of explanation and proof of new ideas and approaches: even those participants who do not choose to delve into the deeper layers in the course materials and reading lists will appreciate knowing there is a credible intellectual hinterland

■ an opportunity to enhance variety (see the five key concepts of training in Chapter 5) by including high content modules (appealing primarily to the 'more intellectual') and very practical modules (appealing primarily to the 'less intellectual').

There is sometimes a problem over pace with very mixed ability classes. People who are very used to assimilating information quickly like to move rapidly from one tutor input and learning module to the next; people who are not so used are more inclined to take their time. I have to say though that in my experience the preference over pace has more to do with broad cultural issues than ability *per se*. For example, I have seen the same appraisal skills workshop completed in half a day, with a group of stockmarket traders (who do not think they are working unless they are rushed) and in three days with a group of research engineers, all of whom had Ph.D.s (and who do not think they are working unless they are going into things in depth). If you are designing for a mixed group, then the best tip is 'vary pace and rhythm' and include extra optional activities for people who work quickly.

Mixed nationality classes

You may recall the training design principle in Chapter 5:

Map the participants' world.

This is the key to designing training for mixed nationality groups. But of course you have to map more than one world. This sounds rather daunting, but in fact the simple dos and don'ts below will be most of what you need:

- *Don't* allow the training to be obviously 'British' (or indeed obviously any one nationality). Use international settings for role plays, case studies from a variety of cultures, and theories from management writers of all nationalities.

- *Do* check how practicalities vary between nationalities and strike a balance. For example, the French will often expect a long lunch; Americans will often want to work through lunch; acknowledge the differences and schedule a one-hour complete break.

- *Don't* assume that everyone will speak fluent English, even when the language of the training – or even the organisation – is English. Allow more time for explanation and discussion. Use simple, and fewer words wherever possible. In my experience, the more mixed the group is in terms of nationality, the more time is needed for each activity.

- *Do* include plenty of opportunity for group discussion, where participants from different nationalities exchange views and experiences. This ensures the training maps as many worlds as there are countries represented.

In brief

■ Because training is usually delivered to groups of people, the training designer needs to bear individual differences in mind if some participants are not to be left out, bored, or alienated.

■ The two key principles in designing for a group are:
  ❑ give participants choices
  ❑ and design training in layers.

■ The most important differences between individuals from the training designer's point of view are those that affect profoundly their approach to and style of learning.

■ The training designer should be aware that people differ greatly on the following four dimensions:
  ❑ extrovert/introvert
  ❑ evidence-seeking/concept-loving
  ❑ logic-led/values-driven
  ❑ structured/fluid.

■ Well-designed training for mixed groups will contain some elements which appeal to both ends of each dimension, and many elements which are presented in a balanced way, not favouring either extreme.

■ Mixed ability classes present a number of opportunities to the training designer to get interesting and informative discussion going between more intellectual and more practical people. Ability of participants in the narrow educational sense is not usually a critical factor in determining the success of a training intervention. The interactive, practical nature of well-designed training allows participants to adapt it to their own preferred level of intellectualisation.

■ It can sometimes be difficult to design training for a group of individuals whose preferred pace of working is very varied. The best tip here is 'vary pace and rhythm'.

■ Mixed nationality classes are a special case of designing training for diversity. The training design must include multiple references to all cultures represented. The simplest way to provide this is through plenty of time for discussion between participants of different nationalities.

8 Classic Training Challenges

Introduction

I hope that in reading this book you have become more confident and resourceful in designing training to meet a variety of training challenges. To bridge the gap between reading and doing, I would like finally to present a handful of training assignments for you to think about tackling. Each assignment has been chosen to be representative of a classic training challenge. After each assignment has been introduced, there is a short set of questions, typical of the questions you would need to reflect on if you embarked on the training design. Each question is followed by a reference to a section in this book where you will find at least part of the answer.

In my experience, the more of a questioning mind the training designer brings to a training assignment, the more effective a training intervention she will create. Because her questioning mind will have roved around issues of context, of participants' state of mind, of outcome and follow-up – rather than just stayed fixed on training content – her training will stand a chance of bringing about real change for the better in the workplace.

So as you read this last chapter, stop after you have read each assignment. What questions are in your mind now? Then look at the questions I have identified. You may have thought of them all, and more. If so, you are more than half way to designing a good piece of training. Finally, you may want to refer to the specified sections of this book. Then you will see how the different aspects of training which we have covered here come together in the integrated design of an effective training intervention.

Training challenge number one: skills training for the unwilling

A large international accountancy firm sent out an invitation to tender for presentation skills training for its 200 most senior partners. The managing partner of the firm was renowned for his charisma and speaking skills. It was his strongly held view that if more of his colleagues had a very high level of presentation skill the firm would win an even higher proportion of the work it bid for. In truth, he had a rather low opinion of his colleagues in this respect. Over the past few months, he had been present at several prospect meetings where senior partners had bored or confused their audience, in his view. Also, he kept hearing that senior partners of rival firms were being invited to speak at international business conferences. He was panicking about his own firm losing ground. This whole area was a bit of an obsession for him, and he was funding the training initiative from his own 'special projects' budget.

Most of the 200 senior partners for whom the training was intended felt mildly annoyed at the managing partner's project. They admired his speaking skills, and felt he was exceptional. For the most part, they put it down to a combination of his extrovert personality and his education in an American high school which prided itself on teaching its pupils not only subjects but also how to present those subjects to others. They recognised he put his abilities to good effect, but really did not see that they all needed to be like him. They would on the whole have described themselves as competent and experienced presenters – maybe without much flair, but then you've either got it or you haven't, haven't you?

The partners were all the more annoyed because the training was scheduled for the busiest part of their year.

They could be out with clients earning fees every day, and even one day's training would 'cost' the firm tens of thousands of pounds, maybe even hundreds of thousands, in lost revenue. They were for the most part practical people, disinclined to sacrifice solid income for some whim about 'vast increase in revenue-earning potential' – and that was how they saw the managing partner's idea.

Still, he was a forceful character, internally as well as externally, and they had all agreed with varying degrees of reluctance to attend a one-day presentation skills workshop in groups of ten at a time.

Key questions for the training designer

Before embarking on designing this piece of training, you would want to ask yourself the following:

■ What is in this training for the participants? How can I build something into this training to make it seem something other than 'satisfying the whim of the senior partner'? (See page 7 for some ideas, pages 15–16 on 'imagining the participants', pages 39–44 on objective-setting.)

■ Is this training too great a challenge to be feasible? (See pages 9–13 on weighing up the training challenge.)

■ How can I demonstrate the practical benefits of the training? (See pages 104–105 for how to design training for 'doubting Thomases'.)

Training challenge number two: training that costs money for an organisation 'on its uppers'

A British engineering research, design and manufacturing company needed to embark on a programme of skills training for all its team leaders and project managers. Without a new set of skills to support the new processes the company had just invested in, there was unlikely to be a future for anyone.

Yet the company was already heavily in the red. Budgets had been slashed to a minimum, and everyone, from the managing director to the janitor, was trying to keep costs down. Unless the designers of the skills training programme were very careful, there would be such resentment at the cost of training that none of the participants' minds would be on learning the skills.

Key questions for the training designer

▮ How can the cost of the training be kept to a minimum?

▮ How can we advertise the fact that the training has been designed in a very cost-effective way? (For ideas on both these questions, see Chapter 2 on background choices in training.)

▮ How can we demonstrate the return on our investment in training, right from the start of each programme? (See page 41 on the use of SMART objectives.)

Training challenge number three: interesting training for the easily bored

The graduates recruited into this merchant bank were some of the brightest and most sought after in the City. And they knew it. Their graduate training programme opened with a three-day residential workshop after they had been at the bank for two months.

They were still flushed with the success of getting a job in this prestigious organisation. They were also very competitive with one another. They had not yet had any vivid experience of the issues and problems at work, having spent two months visiting a variety of departments. In short, they felt they could do anything. They did not need training – they thought.

The bank had tried delaying formal training until the end of the first year. It had, however, experienced a few expensive mistakes and upsets, caused by graduates with no real awareness of how to work co-operatively with others, of how to manage others' perceptions of them, or of how to accept management from someone whom they might consider their intellectual inferior. The bank was sure some kind of training was necessary early on. But the course they had run for the previous year's graduate intake had been a dismal failure. Participants actually read newspapers during some of the sessions, they were so bored; and by the third morning, only half the group were in the training room. The rest were lying in bed with hangovers after an unscheduled party which got somewhat out of hand.

Key questions for the training designer

- What change exactly does the bank want to bring about through the training? (See page 38 for sub-questions to help you get answers to this key question.)
- What kind of individuals are the graduates? What kinds of activities will hold their attention and keep them involved? (See Chapter 7 for ideas on what their learning styles may be.)
- How can a high impact event be designed? (See Table 15 for many ways to grab and keep attention.)
- How can the training be made an integral part of the graduates' success at work? (See Chapter 4 on the politics of training, and particularly pages 47–50 on who should have a say in training design.)

Training challenge number four: working with a group who won't work with each other

The management team of a UK cosmetics company had a problem, and they hoped training would fix it. There were 10 people in the team, only one a woman, and none of them trusted the woman. She had an abrasive, confrontational style which made the others think she was 'out to get them'. There was lack of trust and professional respect more generally in the team, and one or two very vulnerable personalities who needed to be protected against too much open conflict in a group setting. Meetings had deteriorated to a banal exchange of information interspersed with the odd bout of sniping. The leader had told them to find a good training course, go on it, and sort themselves out! I was chosen to design and deliver a two-day teambuilding workshop. I was not looking forward to it.

Key questions for the training designer

▌ Given the history of problems, several team members felt there was little a two-day workshop could achieve. How could I design something they would believe in enough to make an effort? (See Chapter 3 on objective setting, particularly page 34; see the tips in Chapter 5 on commitment and credibility.)

▌ How could the training be designed in a way which changed the way the group interacted? How could it ensure that no one would be inappropriately exposed, or hurt? (See Chapter 6 on process interventions, and particularly pages 89–92.)

▌ The team felt badly about having so many problems. Was there any way the training could be set up as a reward, rather than a punishment? (See pages 22–25 for an idea or two.)

In brief

▌ Having a questioning mind and knowing some of the right questions to ask are the two most important characteristics of a good training designer.

▌ The biggest challenges in training can be addressed if you understand enough about what has happened before and will happen after the training intervention itself.

▌ To design effective training, you need to integrate all the points in this book into a single approach which establishes what is in the training for the participants and gives it to them.

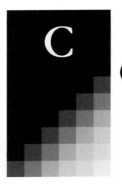

Conclusion

One of the things I like most about designing training is that it can never be perfect. After every single training intervention I have designed, I have thought of ways I could have done it better.

> Would you describe yourself as a self-critical person? Many successful training designers are. But you need to make sure your self-criticism does not lead you into depression. Identify those of your colleagues whom you can rely on to help you keep a sense of perspective, who will stop you thinking that mistakes mean failure.

What you need to exploit this potential for your own development as a training designer is feedback. You yourself need to deliver at least some of the training you design, sit in on courses you have designed which are delivered by someone else, talk to deliverers, participants and customers. Ask people:

■ What worked well?
■ What could have been different and worked better?

Make sure you get both positive comments and constructive criticism. And welcome both.

There is no perfect training intervention, thank goodness, because the variability, ingenuity and unpredictability of people can never be totally accounted for. So make it your habit to criticise the training you have designed, to identify its weak points, to spot the places it fails to engage, convince or communicate.

If you do this, you will design training that is good enough.

Further Reading

DAVIS R, LAWRENCE T, ALEXANDER L T AND YELON S L. *Learning System Design*. Maidenhead, McGraw-Hill, 1974.

GOLDSTEIN I L. *Training in Organisations: Needs assessment, development, and evaluation*. Brooks/Cole, 1986.

HARDINGHAM A AND ROYAL J. *Pulling Together: Teamwork in practice*. London, IPD, 1994.

HONEY P AND MUMFORD A. *The Manual of Learning Styles*. Third edition, Honey, 1986.

HUCZYNSKI A. *Encyclopedia of Management Development Methods*. Aldershot, Gower, 1983.

JUCK B. *Personal Development: Theory and practice in management training*. Chichester, John Wiley, 1983.

KROEGER O AND THUESEN J. *Type Talk at Work*. Delaconte Press, 1992.

LEFRANÇOIS G R. *Psychology for Teaching: A bear always faces the front*. Wadsworth, 1972.

MAGER R F. *Preparing Instructional Objectives*. David S Lake, 1984.

PEDLER M, BURGOYNE J AND BOYDELL T. *A Manager's Guide to Self-development*. Maidenhead, McGraw-Hill, 1978.

ROBINSEN K R. *A Handbook of Training Management*. London, Kogan Page, 1981.

Index

With over 100,000 members, the **Chartered Institute of Personnel and Development** is the largest organisation in Europe dealing with the management and development of people. The Institute operates its own independent publishing unit, producing books and research reports for human resource practitioners and students, and general managers charged with people management responsibilities.

Currently there are some 160 titles in print covering the full range of personnel and development issues. The books have been commissioned from leading experts in the field and are packed with the latest information and guidance to best practice.

For a free copy of the full CIPD Books Catalogue, contact the Publishing Department:

Tel.: 020-8263 3387
Fax: 020-8263 3850
E-mail: publish@cipd.co.uk
Web: www.cipd.co.uk

Orders for books should be sent to Plymbridge Distributors, Estover, Plymouth PL6 7PZ. Tel: 01752 202301. Fax: 01752 202333. (Payment should accompany all orders.)

Other titles in the Training Essentials series

Developing Learning Materials
Jacqui Gough

Today, trainers can draw upon a vast array of learning materials to support their training – from text-based, visual, and audio aids to sophisticated technological resources utilising CBT and multimedia. This comprehensive book covers all the major options. It assesses the advantages, disadvantages, and applications of the different media and gives practical guidance on how to:

- agree learning requirements, set quality standards, and draw up specifications
- brief project teams, printers, and technical producers
- present attractive, well-structured materials to enhance your message
- adapt, modify, and evaluate existing learning materials, or
- design and produce your own – including text-based open learning, participative activities, and IT-based training
- test and pilot your designs.

The sheer range of learning materials can be bewildering but, by following Jacqui Gough's clear survey of the whole field, you will be able to make the right choices, find creative design solutions, and explore less familiar areas with confidence.

Jacqui Gough is an experienced trainer and consultant and runs her own company, Flexible Learning Solutions, which specialises in delivering and producing open and flexible learning materials and courses.

1996 160 pages Paperback ISBN 0 85292 639 1 **£14.99**

Identifying Training Needs
Tom Boydell and Malcolm Leary

Identifying training needs is about matching organisational goals with learning opportunities. This comprehensive book demonstrates why it is important, who is involved, and how to use all the crucial tools and techniques. It covers:

- identifying organisational needs by going beyond current objectives to achieve new targets
- identifying group needs using customer-mapping, and competency and job analysis techniques
- identifying individual needs through performance appraisal, assessment centres, and portfolio development approaches
- assembling information from records, reports, and sources such as interviews, focus groups, and audits
- analysing and presenting the data with cost-benefit comparisons.

By following systematically the guidelines clearly set out in this book, you will ensure that your training remains focused on what your business really needs in order to achieve results.

Tom Boydell and Malcolm Leary have each over 20 years' experience in training and development. They run their own consultancy, Transform, specialising in individual and organisational development, and have written numerous books and articles on a range of training and development topics.

1996 208 pages Paperback ISBN 0 85292 630 8 **£14.99**

Tools for Assessment and Development Centres
Pearn Kandola Occupational Psychologists, Oxford

For better results in selecting, assessing, and developing their staff, forward-looking organisations are relying on assessment and development centres (AC/DCs). Yet, until now, there has been little material available for organisations that want to introduce centres or measure the effectiveness of existing centres. *Tools for Assessment and Development Centres* fills the gap by providing a comprehensive set of accessible, practical, and leading-edge tools to enable managers to develop, implement, and evaluate centres that are:

- relevant to organisational needs
- accurate assessments of performance requirements in the job or role concerned
- fair to participants
- based on best practice.

The package is the result of extensive research in the field by Pearn and Kandola, working with top UK companies; all the tools have been reviewed and trialled by experienced assessment exercise designers and assessment centre users.

The tools are laid out in a systematic 'chain-link model' which fully covers every stage in the construction of AC/DCs. For those new to the process, the links in the chain can be tackled in sequence, top to bottom. Other organisations with established centres will be able to pinpoint existing weak links and, by reference to the relevant set of tools, identify specific problems and take remedial action.

The material is presented as five units: an overview and four sets of tools contained in a polypropylene briefcase:

Overview (spiral-bound book, 32 pages)
A succinct introduction to the 'chain-link model', the development of the tools, practical guidance on using the pack, and further reference sources.

Tools for defining criteria/competencies for assessment centres and development centres (ringbinder, 154 pages)
Eleven tools guide users to defining criteria that relate to the needs of the

organisation and to the demands of current job roles. They show how criteria can be defined and checked through a series of workshops, check-lists, and questionnaires.

Tools for designing assessment exercises (ringbinder, 184 pages)
Seven stages in exercise design are described and supported with 12 tools to make the task easier and quicker, and to ensure that every exercise is appropriate to its intended use and fair to all potential participants.

Tools for preparing people (ringbinder, 244 pages)
This section is divided into two parts: *Preparing assessors* contains seven tools for informing and developing assessors in the required knowledge and skills. *Preparing participants and managers* contains seven tools for briefing managers of AC/DC participants to ensure that those involved are fully committed to, and have a sound understanding of, the purposes of the initiative.

Tools for auditing assessment centres and development centres (ringbinder, 160 pages)
Nine tools provide the key steps for auditing centres to ensure that they make a meaningful and worthwhile contribution to individual and organisational goals.

1996 A4 ISBN 0 85292 631 6 **£500.00**